Student Solutions Manual

for use with

Essentials of Business Statistics

Second Edition

Bruce L. Bowerman
Miami University

Richard T. O'Connell
Miami University

J. B. Orris
Butler University

Dawn C. Porter
University of Southern California

Prepared by
Patrick Schur
Miami University

**McGraw-Hill
Irwin**

Boston Burr Ridge, IL Dubuque, IA Madison, WI New York San Francisco St. Louis
Bangkok Bogotá Caracas Kuala Lumpur Lisbon London Madrid Mexico City
Milan Montreal New Delhi Santiago Seoul Singapore Sydney Taipei Toronto

**McGraw-Hill
Irwin**

Student Solutions Manual for use with
ESSENTIALS OF BUSINESS STATISTICS
Bruce L. Bowerman, Richard T. O'Connell, J. B. Orris and Dawn C. Porter

Published by McGraw-Hill/Irwin, an imprint of The McGraw-Hill Companies, Inc., 1221 Avenue of the Americas, New York, NY 10020. Copyright © 2008 by The McGraw-Hill Companies, Inc. All rights reserved.

1 2 3 4 5 6 7 8 9 0 BKM/BKM 0 9 8 7 6

ISBN: 978-0-07-320856-5
MHID: 0-07-320856-6

www.mhhe.com

Table of Contents

CHAPTER 1—An Introduction to Business Statistics

1.1 A population is a set of existing units.
Consumers utilizing a particular product.

1.3 **a.** Quantitative; dollar amounts correspond to values on the real number line.

    b. Quantitative; net profit is a dollar amount.

    c. Qualitative; which stock exchange is a category.

    d. Quantitative; national debt is a dollar amount.

    e. Qualitative; media is categorized into radio, television, or print.

1.5 **a.** Descriptive statistics: science of describing the important aspects of a set of measurements.

    b. Statistical inference: science of using a sample of measurements to make generalizations about the important aspects of a population of measurements.

    c. Random sample: selected in a manner so that on each selection from the population every unit remaining in the population on that selection has the same chance of being chosen.

    d. Systematic sample: select every nth unit of a population.

1.7 From Table 1.1 (starting in the upper left-hand corner) we obtain the following 2-digit random numbers:

33 03 92 85 08 51 60 94 58 09 14 74 24 87 07

Crossing out numbers greater than 22 (because there are only 22 companies), the sample consists of firms 03, 08, 09, 14, and 07. That is:

03 PepsiCo	09 Archer Daniels
07 General Mills	14 Campbell Soup
08 ConAngra Foods	

1.9 **a.** From Table 1.1 (starting in the upper left-hand corner) we obtain 5-digit random numbers:

33276	03427	~~92737~~	~~85689~~	08178
51259	60268	~~94904~~	58586	09998
14346	~~74103~~	24200	~~87308~~	07351

Crossing out the numbers greater than 73,219 (because there are only 73,219 registration cards), the first ten registration cards in the sample are cards:

33276	03427	08178	51259	60268
58586	09998	14346	24200	07351

    b. Most of the scores would fall between 36 and 48 because 36 is the smallest score in the sample and 48 is the largest score in the sample. An estimate of the proportion of scores that would exceed 42 is $\frac{40}{65} = .615$ because 40 of the 65 sample scores exceed 42.

1.11 **a.** People who oppose TV sex and violence would be most likely to respond. Yes, almost all respondents are concerned about sex, language, and violence.

 b. It is doubtful that a random sample would give the same results. Given the number of people who watch shows containing sex, vulgar language, and violence, it is doubtful that 96 to 97 percent of the population is concerned about sex, language, and violence on TV.

 c. It is highly doubtful that 90% of the general population desires a V-chip.

1.13 A process is in statistical control if it does not exhibit any unusual process variation.

1.15

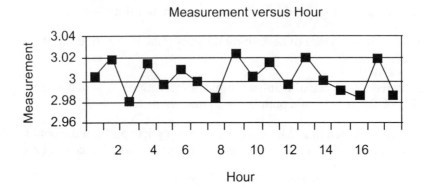

The measurements appear to be in control because there is reasonably constant variation at a horizontal level.

1.17 No, the percentages do not seem to be in control. The plot reveals higher percentages early in the week, which is when most business traveling is done.

1.19 Yes, the waiting times are in control. There is reasonably constant variation at a horizontal level.

1.21 An ordinal variable is a qualitative variable such that there is a meaningful ordering, or ranking, of the categories. A nominal variable is a qualitative variable such that there is no meaningful ordering, or ranking, of the categories.

1.23 Nominative, ordinal, ordinal, ordinal, nominative, and nominative.

1.25 A stratified random sample is selected by dividing the population into some number of strata, and then randomly sampling inside each strata.

 Potential strata: students who live off campus and
  students who live on campus.

1.27 Response Variable: Whether or not a person has lung cancer. Factors: Age, sex, occupation, and number of cigarettes smoked per day. Observational study.

1.29 Sampling error, Nonresponse error, Recording error

1.31 His comments are justified because voluntary response surveys are usually biased.

1.33 Not in statistical control, opinions may vary.

1.35   **a.**   Number the minutes from 00 to 59 and use the random number table to select the randomly selected minutes.

       b.   Hours number 15, 7, 57, 42, and 59.

CHAPTER 2—Descriptive Statistics

2.1 **a.**   Both halves are mirror images of each other and one peak in the middle, tapering on both ends.

      b.   Two distinct high points.

      c.   Having a long tail to the left.

      d.   Having a long tail to the right.

2.3 **a.**

```
Stem-and-Leaf Display of Profit Margin    n = 35
Leaf Unit = 0.10

    Frequency     Stem
            2      1|  1 8
            2      2|  2 9
            6      3|  1 2 3 6 6 9
            4      4|  0 4 7 9
           12      5|  0 0 0 2 3 4 8 9 9 9 9 9
            3      6|  1 8 9
            1      7|  0
            1      8|  6
            1      9|  2
            1     10|  9
            1     11|  2
                  12|
                  13|
                  14|
                  15|
                  16|
                  17|
                  18|
                  19|
                  20|
                  21|
                  22|
                  23|
            1     24|  0
```

Distribution is skewed right.

b. Stem-and-Leaf of Display on Capital   n = 35
   Leaf Unit = 0.10

```
Frequency       Stem
        1          0|  0
                   1|
                   2|
                   3|
        1          4|  0
                   5|
                   6|
                   7|
        2          8|  3 6
        1          9|  2
                  10|
        4         11|  0 2 5 6
        3         12|  6 7 8
        1         13|  1
        3         14|  4 7 7
        3         15|  2 4 9
        1         16|  5
        2         17|  0 6
        1         18|  3
        3         19|  2 7 8
        3         20|  3 6 8
        2         21|  1 7
        1         22|  8
                  23|
                  24|
        2         25|  1 7
                  26|
                  27|
                  28|
                  29|
                  30|
                  31|
                  32|
        1         33|  4
```

Distribution is quite variable, but symmetric with both high and low outliers.

c. Profit margins are skewed to the right and less spread out when compared to Return on Capital.

2.5 **a.** We have $2^6 = 64$ and $2^7 = 128$. Since $2^6 < n = 65$ and $2^7 > n = 65$, we use $K = 7$ classes.

Class length =

$$\frac{\text{largest measurement} - \text{smallest measurement}}{K} = \frac{48 - 36}{7} = \frac{12}{7} = 1.71 \approx 2$$

Class	Frequency	Relative Frequency			Boundaries	Midpoint
36 – 37	1	1/65	=	.0154	35.5, 37.5	36.5
38 – 39	7	7/65	=	.1077	37.5, 39.5	38.5
40 – 41	11	11/65	=	.1692	39.5, 41.5	40.5
42 – 43	14	14/65	=	.2154	41.5, 43.5	42.5
44 – 45	21	21/65	=	.3231	43.5, 45.5	44.5
46 – 47	10	10/65	=	.1538	45.5, 47.5	46.5
48 – 49	1	1/65	=	.0154	47.5, 49.5	48.5

b. The population of all possible customer satisfaction ratings is slightly skewed with a tail to the left.

c. The relative frequency histogram would be the same as the frequency histogram in Figure 2.15, except the heights of the rectangles would be the relative frequencies given in the table of part (a). This means the numbers on the vertical axis in Figure 2.15 – 0, 5, 10, 15, 20, 25 – would be divided by 65. Thus, the numbers on the vertical axis would be 0, .077, .154, .231, .308, .385. Alternatively, if we have MINITAB construct a relative frequency histogram by choosing its own classes, we obtain the following:

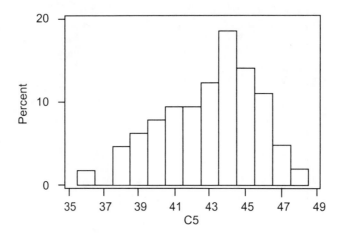

2.7 a. We have $2^5 = 32$ and $2^6 = 64$. Since $2^5 < n = 40$ and $2^6 > n = 40$, we use $K = 6$ classes.

$$\text{Class length} = \frac{\text{largest measurement} - \text{smallest measurement}}{K} = \frac{54.0 - 46.8}{6} = 1.2$$

Class	Frequency	Relative Frequency	Boundaries	Midpoint
46.8 – 47.9	2	.05	46.75, 47.95	47.35
48.0 – 49.1	5	.125	47.95, 49.15	48.55

49.2 – 50.3	11	.275	49.15, 50.35	49.75
50.4 – 51.5	12	.3	50.35, 51.55	50.95
51.6 – 52.7	6	.15	51.55, 52.75	52.15
52.8 – 53.9	3	.075	52.75, 53.95	53.35
54.0 – 55.1*	1	.025	53.95, 55.15	54.55

* Since the largest measurement is not within the sixth class, we add a seventh class.

b. The population of all possible breaking strengths seems symmetrical.

2.9
```
Stem-and-leaf of Days    N = 67
Leaf Unit = 1.0

    4      0  4588
   20      1  1111244445678889
  (15)     2  012333335567799
   32      3  01124555569
   21      4  122357
   15      5  0348
   11      6  47
    9      7  0
    8      8  0135
    4      9  26
    2     10  2
    1     11  1
```

The 61 home runs hit by Maris would be considered an outlier, although an exceptional individual achievement.

2.11 a.

Class	Factor	Height
$50K to 100K	$\frac{100-50}{10-0}=\frac{50}{10}=5$	$\left(\frac{1}{5}\right)(60)=12$
$100K to 150K	$\frac{150-100}{10-0}=\frac{50}{10}=5$	$\left(\frac{1}{5}\right)(24)=4\frac{4}{5}$
$150K to 200K	$\frac{200-150}{10-0}=\frac{50}{10}=5$	$\left(\frac{1}{5}\right)(19)=3\frac{4}{5}$
$200K to 250K	$\frac{250-200}{10-0}=\frac{50}{10}=5$	$\left(\frac{1}{5}\right)(22)=4\frac{2}{5}$
$250K to 500K	$\frac{500-250}{10-0}=\frac{250}{10}=25$	$\left(\frac{1}{25}\right)(21)=\frac{21}{25}$

b, c. Student should sketch the histogram.

2.13 **a.** Population parameter: number calculated using the population measurements that describe some aspect of the population.
Point estimate: a one-number estimate of the value of a population parameter.

b. The sample mean is the point estimate of the population mean.

2.15

	N	MEAN	MEDIAN	MODE
a	10	9.600	10.000	10.00
b	9	103.33	100.00	90.00

2.17 **a.** Yes, because $\bar{x} > 42$.

b. The mean of 42.954 is slightly less than the median of 43.
The stem-and-leaf display shows only slight skewness to the left.

2.19 **a.** Yes, because $\bar{x} > 50$.

b. $\text{median} = \dfrac{50.6 + 50.7}{2} = 50.65$

The mean and median are very similar. The stem-and-leaf display shows very little skewness.

2.21-2.25 MINITAB output for all variables on data comparing lifestyles.

Variable	N	N*	Mean	Median	TrMean	StDev
voters	9	0	70.70	71.50	70.70	11.81
income tax	9	0	49.44	50.00	49.44	7.30
video reentals	8	0	4.03	2.10	4.03	4.49
PCs	8	0	18.94	17.50	18.94	7.10
Religion	6	1	31.65	26.25	31.65	18.21

Variable	SE Mean	Minimum	Maximum	Q1	Q3
voters	3.94	49.10	85.00	61.35	80.40
income t	2.43	40.00	60.00	42.00	55.50
video re	1.59	0.70	13.80	1.13	6.45
PCs	2.51	11.50	35.00	14.50	20.00
Religion	7.43	10.00	55.80	17.50	52.65

2.21 Somewhat skewed left; the U.S. has the lowest percentage.
2.23 Skewed right; U.S. is the highest.
2.25 Skewed right; U.S. is above the mean and median.

2.27 **a.** Skewed to the right. Most players earned the league minimum.

b. Earning more than the mean: about 33%
Earning more than the median: 50%

c. Explanations will vary. All quotes are a distortion/misrepresentation of the true earnings by the majority of players.

2.29 Both the variance and standard deviation measure the spread of the individual values about the mean. The larger the spread, the more variation in the data.

2.31 Used to find intervals that contain a specified percentage of the individual measurements in the population or a bound on the percentage when using Chebyshev's Theorem.

2.33 range = 15 − 5 = 10

$$\sigma^2 = \frac{\sum_{i=1}^{5}(x_i - \mu)^2}{5} = \frac{(5-10)^2 + (8-10)^2 + (10-10)^2 + (12-10)^2 + (15-10)^2}{5}$$

$$= \frac{25 + 4 + 0 + 4 + 25}{5} = 11.6$$

$$\sigma = \sqrt{11.6} = 3.4059$$

2.35 a **Airline Revenues**

Revenue ($ Billions)	Rev − 8.15	Sum of (Rev − 8.15)^2	Sum of (Rev − 8.15)^2	Pop Variance	Pop Std. Dev.
17.4	9.25	85.5625	266.3650	26.6365	5.1611
13.7	5.55	30.8025			
13.3	5.15	26.5225			
9.5	1.35	1.8225			
8.9	0.75	0.5625			
6.8	−1.35	1.8225			
5.9	−2.25	5.0625			
2.4	−5.75	33.0625			
2.3	−5.85	34.2225			
1.3	−6.85	46.9225			
Mean = 8.15					

Revenues:
Mean =   8.15
Range =   16.1
Variance =   26.6365
Std. Dev. =   5.1611

Airline Profits

Profit ($ Millions)	Prof − 244.1	(Rev − 244.1)^2	Sum of (Rev − 244.1)^2	Pop Variance	Pop Std. Dev.
−1228	−983.9	968059.21	11,802,470.9000	1,180,247,0900	1086.3918
−2808	−2563.9	6573583.21			
−773	−528.9	279735.21			
248	492.1	242162.41			
38	282.1	79580.41			
1461	1705.1	2907366.01			
442	686.1	470733.21			
14	258.1	66615.61			
57	301.1	90661.21			
108	352.1	123974.41			
Mean = −244.1					

Profits:
Mean =   -244.1
Range =   4269
Variance =   1,180,247.0900
Std. Dev. =   1086.3918

b.

Airline	Profit	Profit – Mean	z-score
American	−1228	−983.9	−0.906
United	−2808	−2563.9	−2.360
Delta	−773	−528.9	−0.487
Northwest	248	492.1	0.453
Continental	38	282.1	0.260
US Airways	1461	1705.1	1.570
Southwest	442	686.1	0.632
Alaska	14	258.1	0.238
America West	57	301.1	0.277
Express Jet	108	352.1	0.324

Most airlines' profits are within two standard deviations of the mean with the exception of United Airlines.

2.37   a.   The stem-and-leaf display and the histogram indicate that the breaking strengths are approximately normally distributed. Therefore, the empirical rule is appropriate.

b.   68.26%: [50.575 ± 1(1.6438)] = [48.9312, 52.2188]
     95.44%: [50.575 ± 2(1.6438)] = [47.2875, 53.8626]
     99.73%: [50.575 ± 3(1.6438)] = [45.6436, 55.5064]

c.   We estimate that the breaking strengths of 99.73% of the trashbags are between 45.6436 lbs and 55.5064 lbs. Thus, almost any trashbag will have a breaking strength that exceeds 45 lbs.

d.   27 out of 40 (or 67.5%) actually fall within the interval $[\bar{x} \pm s]$.
     38 out of 40 (or 95%) actually fall within the interval $[\bar{x} \pm 2s]$.
     40 out of 40 (or 100%) actually fall within the interval $[\bar{x} \pm 3s]$.
     These percentages compare favorably with those given by the Empirical Rule (68.26%, 95.44%, and 99.73%). This suggests that our inferences are valid.

2.39   a.   It is somewhat reasonable.

b. $[\bar{x} \pm s] = [42.95 \pm 2.6424] = [40.3076, 45.5924]$
     $[\bar{x} \pm 2s] = [42.95 \pm 2(2.6424)] = [37.6652, 48.2348]$
     $[\bar{x} \pm 3s] = [42.95 \pm 3(2.6424)] = [35.0228, 50.8772]$

c.   Yes, because the lower limit of the interval is greater than 35.

d.   63% fall into $[\bar{x} \pm s]$, 98.46% fall into $[\bar{x} \pm 2s]$, 100% fall into $[\bar{x} \pm 3s]$.
     Yes, they are reasonably valid.

2.41 **a.**

RS Internet Age Fund:	$[10.93 - 2*41.96, 10.93 + 2*41.96] = [-72.99, 94.85]$	
Franklin Income A Fund:	$[13 - 2*9.36, 13 + 2*9.36] = [-5.72, 31.72]$	
Jacob Internet Fund:	$[34.45 - 2*41.16, 34.5 + 2*41.16] = [-47.87, 116.77]$	

b. RS has the lowest average and highest variability.
Franklin has the second lowest average and the smallest variability.
Jacob has the highest average return and the second highest variability.

c.

RS Internet Age Fund:	Coefficient of Variation = 41.96 / 10.93 * 100 = 383.9%
Franklin Income A Fund:	Coefficient of Variation = 9.36 / 13 * 100 = 72%
Jacob Internet Fund:	Coefficient of Variation = 41.14 / 34.45 * 100 = 119.4%

RS Internet is riskiest, Jacob is second and Franklin is least risky.

2.43 **a.** The value such that a specified percentage of the measurements in a population or sample fall at or below it.

b. A value below which approximately 25% of the measurements lie

c. The 75th percentile

d. $IQR = Q_3 - Q_1$ contains the middle 50% of the data.

2.45

		Customer Satisfaction	Waiting Times	Trash Bags
a.	90th percentile	46	8.9	52.8
b.	median	43	5.25	50.65
c.	Q1	41	3.8	49.45
d.	Q3	45	7.2	51.65
e.	10th percentile	39	2.25	48.4
f.	IQR	4	3.4	2.15

Five Number Summary:

	Customer Satisfaction	Waiting Times	Trash Bags
lowest	36	0.4	46.8
Q1	41	3.8	49.45
median	43	5.25	50.65
Q3	45	7.2	51.6
highest	48	11.6	54.0

Box-and-Whisker Displays:

Customer Satisfaction:

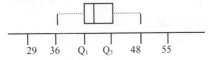

$$\begin{array}{cccccc} 29 & 36 & Q_1 & Q_3 & 48 & 55 \end{array}$$

Waiting Times:

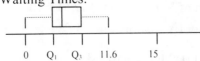

$$\begin{array}{ccccc} 0 & Q_1 & Q_3 & 11.6 & 15 \end{array}$$

Trash Bags:

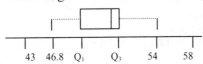

$$\begin{array}{cccccc} 43 & 46.8 & Q_1 & Q_3 & 54 & 58 \end{array}$$

2.47 Overall, the thirty-year rates are higher than the 15-year rates. The variability is similar. Average of the differences = .4444

2.49 **a.** All categories showed improvement.

b. Most: strategic quality planning, quality and operational results
Least: information and analysis, human resource development and management

c. Increase: leadership, human resource development, customer focus and satisfaction
Decrease: strategic quality planning, management of process quality
Others stayed about the same.

d. The skewness changed in leadership, strategic quality planning, human resource development, and quality and operational results.

2.51 Examples and analyses will vary.

2.53

	'97	'05
GM	32.0	28.35
Chrysler	10.4	12.79
Ford	18.0	20.67
Japanese	31.1	24.11
Other	8.5	14.08

Ford, Chrysler, and other imports have gained share from GM and Japanese.

2.55 **a.** $\hat{p} = \dfrac{111}{205} = .541$

b. Since the point estimate of .541 is greater than .5, this sample result provides some evidence that a majority disapprove of the actions taken. Whether this evidence is convincing will be discussed in later chapters.

2.57

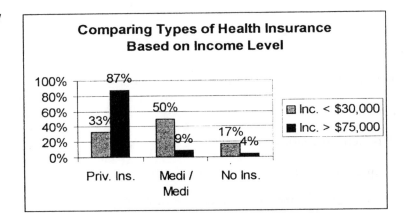

2.59   Data are scattered around a straight line with positive slope.

2.61   Scatter plot: each value of y is plotted against its corresponding value of x.
Runs plot: a graph of individual process measurements versus time

2.63

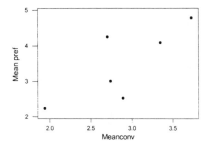

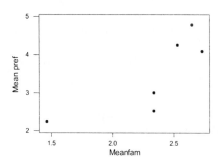

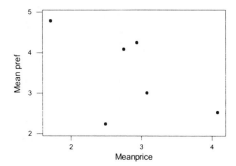

2.65 Examples and reports will vary.

2.67 **a.** No, very slight (if any).

b. Yes, strong trend.

c. The line graph is more appropriate.

d. Probably not; explanations will vary.

2.69 The midpoint equals the average of the measurements in the class.

2.71 **a.**
$$\mu = \frac{100,000(10.7) + 500,000(21.7) + 500,000(9.9) + 200,000(5.8) + 50,000(5.5)}{100,000 + 500,000 + 500,000 + 200,000 + 50,000}$$

$$\mu = \frac{18,305,000}{1,350,000} = 13.56\%$$

b. unweighted mean = 10.72%

More money was invested in funds with larger gains.

2.73 **a.** $\bar{x} = \dfrac{53(2) + 118(5) + 21(8) + 3(11)}{195} = 4.6lbs$

b. $s^2 = \dfrac{53(2 - 4.6)^2 + 118(5 - 4.6)^2 + 21(8 - 4.6)^2 + 3(11 - 4.6)^2}{195 - 1} = \dfrac{742.8}{194} = 3.829$

2.75

Midpoint	Freq	M*f	(M – mean)**2	F*diff^2
30	1	30	462.25	462.25
35	3	105	272.25	816.75
40	3	120	132.25	396.75
45	13	585	42.25	549.25
50	14	700	2.25	31.5
55	12	660	12.25	147
60	9	540	72.25	650.25
65	1	65	182.25	182.25
70	3	210	342.25	1026.75
75	1	75	552.25	552.25

sample mean = 51.5   variance = 81.61017
s = 9.033835

2.77 Yes, the ending value is $I(1+R_g)^n$, where I is the initial investment.

2.79 $1,000,000(1+R_g)^4 = 4,000,000$

$$(1+R_g)^4 = 4$$

$$(1+R_g) = \sqrt[4]{4}$$

$$R_g = 1.4142 - 1$$

$$R_g = .4142$$

2.81 **a.** 1990–95: $\dfrac{1096 - 789}{7891} = .3891$

1995–2000: $\dfrac{1534 - 1096}{1096} = .3996$

$R_g = \sqrt{(1.3891)(1.3996)} - 1 = .39434$

b. $\dfrac{x - 1534}{1534} = .39434$

$x = \$2,139$

2.83 Explanations will vary.

2.85 Graphs not shown. The best graphs for this data would be bar charts.

Explanations will vary.

2.87 **a.** $538 \pm 3(41) = 538 \pm 123 = [415, 661]$

b. Yes, it is beyond the interval.

2.89 The graph indicates that Chevy trucks far exceed Ford and Dodge in terms of resale value, but the y-axis scale is misleading.

2.91 **a.**

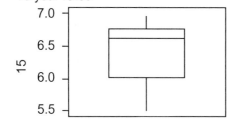 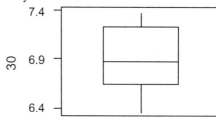

b. fixed rates vs variable rates

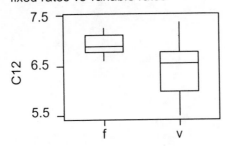

c. 15 year rates: fixed vs variable   30 year rates: fixed vs variable

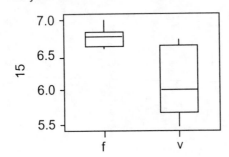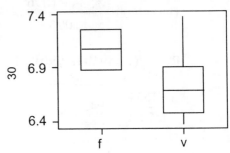

CHAPTER 3—Probability

3.1 Experiment—Any process of observation that has an uncertain outcome.

Event—A set of sample space outcomes.

Probability—The probability of an event is the sum of the probabilities of the sample space outcomes.

Sample Space—The set of all possible experimental outcomes.

3.3 **a.**

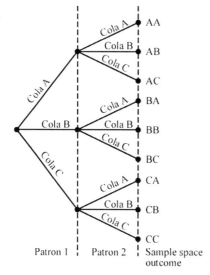

Patron 1   Patron 2   Sample space outcome

b. (1) *AA*
(2) *AA, BB, CC*
(3) *AB, AC, BA, BC, CA, CB*
(4) *AA, AB, AC, BA, CA*
(5) *AA, AB, BA, BB*

c. Each outcome has probability $\frac{1}{9}$.

(1) $\frac{1}{9}$

(2) $3\left(\frac{1}{9}\right) = \frac{1}{3}$

(3) $6\left(\frac{1}{9}\right) = \frac{2}{3}$

(4) $5\left(\frac{1}{9}\right) = \frac{5}{9}$

(5) $4\left(\frac{1}{9}\right) = \frac{4}{9}$

3.5 **a.** Sample space outcomes:
PPPP, PPPN, PPNP, PPNN, PNPP, PNPN, PNNP, PNNN, NPPP, NPPN, NPNP, NPNN, NNPP, NNPN, NNNP, NNNN

    b.   (1) *PPPN, PPNP, PNPP, NPPP*
            (2) *PPNN, PNPN, PNNP, PNNN, NPPN, NPNP, NPNN, NNPP, NNPN, NNNP, NNNN*
            (3) All outcomes except *NNNN*
            (4) *PPPP, NNNN*

    c.   Each outcome has probability $\dfrac{1}{16}$

$$(1)\ 4\left(\frac{1}{16}\right)=\frac{1}{4}$$

$$(2)\ 11\left(\frac{1}{16}\right)=\frac{11}{16}$$

$$(3)\ 15\left(\frac{1}{16}\right)=\frac{15}{16}$$

$$(4)\ 2\left(\frac{1}{16}\right)=\frac{1}{8}$$

3.7   The sum of the probabilities of the individual outcomes sum to 1.
       $P(E) = 1 - (.2 + .15 + .3 + .2) = .15$

3.9   Complement of A: Event A does not occur

       A U B: the union of events A and B (A <u>or</u> B)

       A B: the intersection of events A and B (A <u>and</u> B)

       A B: Event A does not occur and Event B does not occur

3.11   **a.**   (1) $P(M)=\dfrac{2,500}{10,000}=.25$

               (2) $P(V)=\dfrac{4,000}{10,000}=.40$

               (3) $P(M\cap V)=\dfrac{1,000}{10,000}=.10$

    b.

	M	$\overline{M}$	Total
V	1,000	3,000	4,000
$\overline{V}$	1,500	4,500	6,000
Total	2,500	7,500	10,000

    c.   (1) $P(M\cup V)=P(M)+P(V)-P(M\cap V)=.25+.40-.10=.55$

            (2) $P(\overline{M}\cap\overline{V})=\dfrac{4,500}{10,000}=.45$

            (3) $P(M\cap\overline{V})+P(\overline{M}\cap V)=.15+.30=.45$

3.13 **a.** $\dfrac{25}{40} = \dfrac{5}{8}$

      b. $\dfrac{6+15}{40} = \dfrac{21}{40}$

      c. $\dfrac{9+10}{40} = \dfrac{19}{40}$

      d. $\dfrac{15}{40} = \dfrac{3}{8}$

      e. $\dfrac{15+10}{40} + \dfrac{6+15}{40} - \dfrac{15}{40} = \dfrac{31}{40}$

3.15 **a.** $\dfrac{668{,}100 + 531{,}800 + 505{,}100}{8{,}300{,}000} = .205$

      b. $1 - \dfrac{668{,}100 + 531{,}800 + 505{,}100 + 418{,}200 + 386{,}500}{8{,}300{,}000} = 1 - .302 = .698$

      c. $1 - .302 - \dfrac{383{,}500 + 378{,}500}{8{,}300{,}000} = 1 - .302 - .092 = .606$

      d. $\dfrac{418{,}200 + 386{,}500 + \cdots + 299{,}500}{8{,}300{,}000} = .303$

3.17 Events are independent if the outcome of one does not affect the outcome of the other.

3.19 **a.** $\dfrac{9}{15} = .6$

      b. $\dfrac{10}{25} = .4$

      c. Dependent. For two events to be independent, $P(\text{Aero} \mid \text{Low}) = P(\text{Aero})$

      $P(\text{Aero} \mid \text{Low}) = 2/7$ but the $P(\text{Aero}) = 3/8$. They are not equal.

3.21 .55, $P(\text{John}) + P(\text{Jane}) - P(\text{John} \cap \text{Jane}) = .4 + .5 - .35 = .55$

3.23 $P(\text{Aware}) = .47$, $P(\text{Prog/Aware}) = .36$

In order to program, the parent must be aware their set has a V-chip.

$P(\Pr og \cap Aware) = P(Aware)P(\Pr og \mid Aware) = (.47)(.36) = .1692$

3.25 $P(\text{MBA} \cup \text{Manager}) = P(\text{MBA}) + P(\text{Manager}) - P(\text{MBA} \cap \text{Manager})$
      $= .25 + .15 - .09 = .31$

3.27 **a.**

	Fire	~~Fire~~	Total
Fraud	16	24	40
$\overline{\text{Fraud}}$	24	36	60
Total	40	60	100

b. $P(\text{Fraud}|\text{Fire}) = \dfrac{16}{40} = .4$

c. Yes; $P(\text{Fraud}|\text{Fire}) = \dfrac{16}{40} = .4 = P(\text{Fraud})$

3.29 **a.** $P(D1 \cap D2) = P(D1)P(D2) = (.95)(.92) = .874$

b. $P(D1 \cup D2) = P(D1) + P(D2) - P(D1 \cap D2) = .95 + .92 + .874 = .996$

c. $1 - P(D1 \cup D2) = 1 - .996 = .004$

3.31 **a.** $P(\text{KPWR}|3 - 7\,\text{PM}) = .10$

b. $P(\text{KLAX}|3 - 7\,\text{PM}) = .059$
$P(\text{KROQ}|3 - 7\,\text{PM}) = .068$
$P(\text{KIIS}|3 - 7\,\text{PM}) = .049$
$P(\text{KFI}|3 - 7\,\text{PM}) = .037$

c. $(.1)(.256) = .0256$

d. KLAX: $(.059)(.256) = .0151$
KROQ: $(.068)(.256) = .0174$
KIIS: $(.049)(.256) = .0125$
KFI: $(.037)(.256) = .0095$

e. $.0256 + .0151 + .0174 + .0125 + .0095 = .0801$

3.33 **a.** $P(\text{none saw cut}) = (.9)^{22} \cdot (.5)^{1} \cdot (.6)^{1} = .0295$

b. $1 - P(\text{none saw cut}) = 1 - .0295 = .9705$

c. Probably not

d. Explanations will vary.

3.35 To update probabilities based on new information.

3.37 $P(A_1|B) = \dfrac{(.2)(.02)}{(.2)(.02)+(.5)(.05)+(.3)(.04)} = .098,\ P(A_2|B)$

$= \dfrac{(.5)(.05)}{(.2)(.02)+(.5)(.05)+(.3)(.04)} = .610,\ P(A_3|B) = \dfrac{(.3)(.04)}{(.2)(.02)+(.5)(.05)+(.3)(.04)} = .292$

3.39 **a.** $P(\text{default}\,|\,\text{late}) = \dfrac{(.03)(.95)}{(.03)(.95)+(.97)(.3)} = .089$

     b. No

3.41 $P(\text{specialist } 1\,|\,\text{incorrect}) = \dfrac{(.3)(.03)}{(.3)(.03)+(.45)(.05)+(.25)(.02)} = .247$

$P(\text{specialist } 2\,|\,\text{incorrect}) = \dfrac{(.45)(.05)}{(.3)(.03)+(.45)(.05)+(.25)(.02)} = .616$

$P(\text{specialist } 3\,|\,\text{incorrect}) = \dfrac{(.25)(.02)}{(.3)(.03)+(.45)(.05)+(.25)(.02)} = .137$

3.43

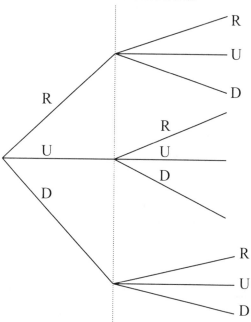

First Stock   Second Stock

3.45 Both stocks rise: P(A rises)*P(B rises) = (.6)(.6) = .36
Both stocks decline: P(A decline)*P(B decline) = (.3)(.3) = .09
Exactly one declines:
P(A+ ∩ B−) + P(A unchanged ∩ B−) + P(A− ∩ B+) + P(A− ∩ B unchanged) =
[(.6)(.3) + (.1)(.3) + (.3)(.6) + (.3)(.1)] = .42

3.47 $P(\text{offered internship} \mid \text{good interview}) = \dfrac{(.4)(.9)}{(.4)(.9)+(.6)(.5)} = .5455$

3.49   P{CLF | BD} = (921 + 55)/1081 = 976/1081 = 0.9029

3.51   P{EMP | (CLF and BD)} = 921/(921 + 55) = 921/976 = 0.9436

3.53   P(violence increased) = 721/1000 = .721

3.55   P(violence increased ∪ quality declined) = 362/1000 = .362

3.57   P(quality declined | violence increased) = .362 /.721 = .502

3.59   Slight dependence: P(violence increased) = .721 vs. P(violence increased | quality declined) = .797 They are close but not equal.

3.61   **a.**   P(purchased | recalled seeing ad) = .13 / .41 = .317

   b.   Yes, since the P(purchased) is less than the P(purchased | recalled seeing ad). The ad did work. If the ad had been ineffective, these two probabilities would have been equal.

3.63   P([5]|T) = P([5])P(T|[5]) / P(T) = (.18)(.00) / (.17) = 0

   P([4]|T) = P([4])P(T|[4]) / P(T) = (.27)(.04) / (.17) = .0635

   P([3]|T) = P([3])P(T|[3]) / P(T) = (.28)(.25) / (.17) = .4118

   P([2]|T) = P([2])P(T|[2]) / P(T) = (.08)(.25) / (.17) = .1176

   P([1]|T) = P([1])P(T|[1]) / P(T) = (.10)(.70) / (.17) = .4118

3.65   P([4]|fam) = P([4]) / P(fam) = .27 / .91 = .2967
   P([3]|fam) = P([3]) / P(fam) = .28 / .91 = .3077
   P([2]|fam) = P([2]) / P(fam) = .08 / .91 = .0879
   P([1]|fam) = P([1]) / P(fam) = .10 / .91 = .1099

3.67   **a.**   P(Alaska delayed) = 501 / 3775 = .1327
   P(America West delayed) = 787 / 7225 = .1089
   America West has a smaller percent of flights delayed.

   b.   P(Alaska|LA) = .1109   P(America West| LA) = .1443
   P(Alaska|Phoenix) = .0515   P(America West| LA) = .0790
   P(Alaska|San Diego) = .0862   P(America West| LA) = .1451
   P(Alaska|San Francisco) = .1686   P(America West| LA) = .2873
   P(Alaska|Seattle) = .1421   P(America West| LA) = .2328
   Alaska Airlines has a smaller percent of flights delayed at each airport.

   c.   Explanations will vary, but answers should discuss the difference in the overall number of flights for each airline and that America West's hub is Phoenix, while Alaskan Airlines' hub is Seattle, where weather plays a more important factor.

CHAPTER 4—Discrete Random Variables

4.1 A random variable is a variable that assumes numerical values determined by the outcome of an experiment.

4.3 a. Discrete
b. Discrete
c. Continuous
d. Discrete
e. Discrete
f. Continuous
g. Continuous

4.5 The probability of each possible outcome is ≥ 0, and the sum of the probabilities of all possible outcomes is 1.

4.7 The standard deviation measures the spread of the population of the random variable.

4.9 a. $\mu_x = 0(.2) + 1(.8) = .8$

$\sigma_x^2 = (0 - .8)^2(.2) + (1 - .8)^2(.8) = .16$

$\sigma_x = \sqrt{.16} = 0.4$

b. $\mu_x = \sum_{\text{all } x} xp(x) = 0(.25) + 1(.45) + 2(.2) + 3(.1) = 1.15$

$\sigma_x^2 = (0 - 1.15)^2(.25) + (1 - 1.15)^2(.45) + (2 - 1.15)^2(.2) + (3 - 1.15)^2(.1) = .8275$

$\sigma_x = \sqrt{.8275} = .9097$

c. $\mu_x = -2(.1) + 0(.3) + 2(.4) + 5(.2) = 1.6$

$\sigma_x^2 = (-2 - 1.6)^2(.1) + (0 - 1.6)^2(.3) + (2 - 1.6)^2(.4) + (5 - 1.6)^2(.2) = 4.44$

$\sigma_x = \sqrt{4.44} = 2.1071$

Since the probabilities sum to 1.00, u_x is the mean of all possible observed values of x.

4.11   **a.**

$$\mu_x = 0\left(\frac{4}{9}\right) + 1\left(\frac{4}{9}\right) + 2\left(\frac{1}{9}\right) = .667$$

$$\sigma_x^2 = \left(0 - .\overline{6}\right)^2\left(\frac{4}{9}\right) + \left(1 - .\overline{6}\right)^2\left(\frac{4}{9}\right) + \left(2 - .\overline{6}\right)^2\left(\frac{1}{9}\right) = .444$$

$$\sigma_x = \sqrt{.444} = .667$$

$[\mu_x \pm 2\sigma_x] = [.667 \pm 2(.667)] = [-.667, 2.001]$ contains at least $\frac{3}{4}$ of the observed values of x.
$[\mu_x \pm 3\sigma_x] = [.667 \pm 3(.667)] = [-1.334, 2.668]$ contains at least $\frac{8}{9}$ of the observed values of x.

b.   See the methods outlined in part a.
$\mu_x = 1.5$
$\sigma_x^2 = .75$
$\sigma_x = .866$
$[\mu_x \pm 2\sigma_x] = [-.232, 3.232]$
$[\mu_x \pm 3\sigma_x] = [-1.098, 4.098]$

c.   See the methods outlined in part (a).
$\mu_x = 2$
$\sigma_x^2 = 1$
$\sigma_x = 1$
$[\mu_x \pm 2\sigma_x] = [0, 4]$
$[\mu_x \pm 3\sigma_x] = [-1, 5]$

4.13   **a.**   Graph not included in this manual.

b. $\mu_x = (-40,000)(.25) + (10,000)(.7) + (70,000)(.05) = \$500$

If numerous oil wells were dug, the average profit would be $500.

4.15   **a.**

x	$400	-$49,600
$p(x)$	.995	.005

b. $\mu_x = 400(.995) + -49,600(.005) = \$150$

c. $x(.995) + (x - 50,000)(.005) = 1,000$
$x - 250 = 1,000$
$x = \$1,250$

4.17 Be sure to account for the cost of the ticket.

$$\mu_x = 12{,}990\left(\frac{1}{5000}\right) + 2{,}990\left(\frac{2}{5000}\right) + 390\left(\frac{5}{5000}\right) + 10\left(\frac{50}{5000}\right) - 10\left(\frac{4942}{5000}\right)$$

$$\mu_x = -\$5.60$$

4.19 **a.**

x	1	2	3	4	5
$p(x)$	.1099	.0879	.3077	.2967	.1978

b. $\mu_x = 1(.1099) + 2(.0879) + \cdots + 5(.1978) = 3.38$

4.21 Values of x are the different possible numbers of successes in n trials.

4.23 MTB > pdf;
    SUBC> binom 5 .3.

```
           BINOMIAL WITH N =    5   P = 0.300000
              K                P( X = K)
              0                  0.1681
              1                  0.3601
              2                  0.3087
              3                  0.1323
              4                  0.0284
              5                  0.0024
```

    MTB > cdf;
    SUBC> binom 5 .3.

```
           BINOMIAL WITH N =    5   P = 0.300000
              K     P( X LESS OR = K)
              0                  0.1681
              1                  0.5282
              2                  0.8369
              3                  0.9692
              4                  0.9976
              5                  1.0000
```

a. $p(x) = \dfrac{5!}{x!(5-x)!}(.3)^x(.7)^{5-x}$

$x = 0, 1, 2, 3, 4, 5$

b. $p(0) = .1681, p(1) = .3601, p(2) = .3087, p(3) = .1323, p(4) = .0284, p(5) = .0024$

c. $P(x = 3) = .1323$

d. $P(x \le 3) = .9692$

e. $P(x < 3) = P(x \le 2) = .8369$

f. $P(x \ge 4) = 1 - P(x \le 3) = 1 - .9692 = .0308$

g. $P(x > 2) = 1 - P(x \leq 2) = 1 - .8369 = .1631$

h. $\mu_x = \sum_{All\,x} xp(x) = 0(.1681) + 1(.3601) + 2(.3087) + 3(.1323) + 4(.0284) + 5(.0024) = 1.5$

$\mu_x = np = 5(.3) = 1.5$

$\sigma_x^2 = \sum_{All\,x} (x - \mu_x)^2 p(x)$

$\quad = (0 - 1.5)^2(.1681) + (1 - 1.5)^2(.3601) + (2 - 1.5)^2(.3087)$

$\qquad\qquad\qquad + (3 - 1.5)^2(.1323) + (4 - 1.5)^2(.0284) + (5 - 1.5)^2(.0024)$

$\quad = 1.05$

$\sigma_x^2 = npq = 5(.3)(.7) = 1.05$

$\sigma_x = \sqrt{\sigma_x^2} = \sqrt{1.05} = 1.024695$

$\sigma_x = \sqrt{npq} = \sqrt{5(.3)(.7)} = 1.024695$

i. $[\mu_x \pm 2\sigma_x] = [1.5 \pm 2(1.024695)] = [-.54939, 3.54939]$

$P(-.54939 \leq x \leq 3.54939) = P(x \leq 3) = .9692$

4.25 a. $p(x) = \dfrac{15!}{x!(15-x)!}(.9)^x(.1)^{15-x}$

b. (1) $P(x \leq 13) = .4509$
(2) $P(x > 10) = 1 - P(x \leq 10) = 1 - .0127 = .9873$
(3) $P(x \geq 14) = 1 - P(x \leq 13) = 1 - .4509 = .5491$
(4) $P(9 \leq x \leq 12) = .0019 + .0105 + .0428 + .1285 = .1837$
(5) $P(x \leq 9) = .0022$

c. No, if the claim is true, then $P(x \leq 9)$ is very small.

4.27 a. $p(x) = \dfrac{4!}{x!(4-x)!}(.5)^x(.5)^{4-x}$

Compute the pdf and cdf in MINITAB using $n = 4$ and $p = .5$.
(1) $P(x = 0) = .0625$
(2) $P(x > 2) = 1 - P(x \leq 2) = 1 - .6875 = .3125$

b. Compute the pdf and cdf in MINITAB using $n = 20$ and $p = .50$
(1) $P(x \leq 9) = .4119$
(2) $P(x > 11) = 1 - P(x \leq 11) = 1 - .7483 = .2517$
(3) $P(x < 5) = .0059$

c. No, if the claim is true, then the probability of fewer than 5 is very small (.0059).

4.29 a. Binomial with $n = 25$, $p = \dfrac{1}{60,000} = .000016\overline{6}$

$P(x = 0) = .9996$
$P(x \geq 1) = 1 - P(x = 0) = .0004$

b. Binomial with $n = 25$, $p = \dfrac{1}{35} = .0285714$

$P(x = 0) = .4845$
$P(x \geq 1) = 1 - .4845 = .5155$

c. $p = \dfrac{1}{35}$

d. $P(0) = \dfrac{25!}{0!(25-0)!}(p)^0 (q)^{25-0} = .999$

$\dfrac{25!}{25!} p^0 q^{25} = .999$

$q^{25} = .999$
$q = (.999)^{1/25}$
$q = .999959981$
$p = 1 - .999959981 = .000040019$

4.31 The probability of an event's occurrence is the same for any two time intervals of equal length.

Whether the event occurs in a time interval is independent of whether the event occurs in any other nonoverlapping interval.

4.33 **a.** $\mu_x = \mu = 2, \sigma_x^2 = \mu = 2, \sigma_x = \sqrt{2} = 1.414$

b. $[\mu_x \pm 2\sigma_x] = [2 \pm 2(1.414)] = [-.828, 4.828]$
$P(-.828 \leq x \leq 4.828) = P(x \leq 4) = .9473$
$[\mu_x \pm 3\sigma_x] = [2 \pm 3(1.414)] = [-2.242, 6.242]$
$P(-2.424 \leq x \leq 6.242) = P(x \leq 6) = .9954$

4.35 **a.** Compute the cdf in MINITAB with $\mu = 4$; $P(x \leq 5) = .7851$

b. Use the results from part (a); $P(x > 5) = 1 - P(x \leq 5) = 1 - .7851 = .2149$

c. Compute the cdf in MINITAB with $\mu = 8$; $P(x \leq 5) = .1912$

d. Compute the cdf in MINITAB with $\mu = 6$; $P(x > 12) = 1 - P(x \leq 12) = 1 - .9912 = .0088$

4.37 Compute the cdf in MINITAB with $\mu = 1.8$.

a. $P(x \geq 10) = 1 - P(x \leq 9) = 1 - 1.000 = 0$; Approximately zero

b. The hospital's rate of comas is unusually high.

4.39 **a.**

x	0	1	2
$p(x)$	$\frac{4}{9}$	$\frac{4}{9}$	$\frac{1}{9}$

b.

x	0	1	2
$p(x)$	.16	.48	.36

c.

x	0	1	2
$p(x)$	.12	.56	.32

4.41 **a.** $\mu_x = 0\left(\dfrac{4}{9}\right) + 1\left(\dfrac{4}{9}\right) + 2\left(\dfrac{1}{9}\right) = \dfrac{2}{3}$

$\sigma_x = \sqrt{\left(0 - \dfrac{2}{3}\right)^2\left(\dfrac{4}{9}\right) + \left(1 - \dfrac{2}{3}\right)^2\left(\dfrac{4}{9}\right) + \left(2 - \dfrac{2}{3}\right)^2\left(\dfrac{1}{9}\right)} = \dfrac{2}{3}$

b. $\mu_x = 1.2, \ \sigma_x = .693$

c. $\mu_x = 1.2, \ \sigma_x = 0.632$

d. 4.39 b & c

e. 4.39 b

4.43 **a.**

x	30,000	−15,000
$p(x)$	.6	.4

$\mu_x = 30,000(.6) - 15,000(.4) = \$12,000$

b. At least $6,000

4.45 **a.** Binomial, $n = 8, p = .8$

b. $P(x \le 3) = .0104$

c. No; if the claim is true, the probability of 3 or fewer being relieved is very small.

4.47 Poisson Distribution with $\mu = 3$

a. $P(x = 0) = \dfrac{e^{-3}\left(3^0\right)}{0!} = .0498$

b. $P(x \le 8) = .9962$

c. $1 - P(x \le 8) = .0038$

d. Poisson with $\mu = 6$
$P(x \le 10) = .9574$

e. Poisson with $\mu = 9$
$P(x \le 5) = .1157$

4.49   Binomial, n = 4, p = .85

   $P (x \geq 1) = 1 - P(x < 1) = 1 - .0005 = .9995$

4.51 $P(x \leq 17) = .3232$

   Not much evidence against it.

4.53   Poisson Distribution with $\mu = 10$

   $P(x \leq 4) = .0293$

   Claim is probably not true.

CHAPTER 5—Continuous Random Variables

5.1 Intervals of values.

5.3 $f(x) \geq 0$ for all x; area under the curve equals 1.

5.5 When a variable has a rectangular distribution over a certain interval.

5.7 $f(x) = \dfrac{1}{d-c} = \dfrac{1}{175-50} = \dfrac{1}{125}$

5.9   **a.** $\mu_x = \dfrac{c+d}{2} = \dfrac{0+6}{2} = 3$

$\sigma_x^2 = \dfrac{(d-c)^2}{12} = \dfrac{(6-0)^2}{12} = 3$

$\sigma_x = \sqrt{3} = 1.732$

b. $[\mu_x \pm \sigma_x] = [3 \pm 1.732] = [1.268, 4.732]$

$P(1.268 \leq x \leq 4.732) = (4.732 - 1.268)\left(\dfrac{1}{6}\right) = .5773$

5.11   **a.**   for $120 \leq x \leq 140$

$f(x) = \dfrac{1}{d-c} = \dfrac{1}{140-120} = \dfrac{1}{20}$

b.
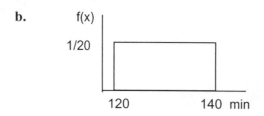

c. $P(125 \leq x \leq 135) = 10\,(1/20) = .5$

d. $P(x \geq 135) = 5\,(1/20) = .25$

5.13 $f(x) = \dfrac{1}{d-c} \Big/ \dfrac{1}{2} = \dfrac{1}{17-5} \Big/ \dfrac{1}{2} = \dfrac{2}{12} = \dfrac{1}{6}$

5.15   **a.** $\mu_x = \dfrac{c+d}{2} = \dfrac{3+6}{2} = 4.5$

b. $\sigma_x = \dfrac{d-c}{\sqrt{12}} = \dfrac{6-3}{\sqrt{12}} = .8660$

$[\mu_x \pm 2\sigma_x] = [4.5 \pm 2(.8660)] = [2.768, 6.232]$

$P(2.768 \le x \le 6.232) = P(3 \le x \le 6) = 1$

$[\mu_x \pm \sigma_x] = [4.5 \pm .8660] = [3.634, 5.366]$

$P(3.634 \le x \le 5.366) = (5.366 - 3.634)\left(\dfrac{1}{3}\right) = .5773$

5.17 a. center

b. spread

5.19 Subtract the mean and divide the result by the standard deviation; tells us the number of standard deviations the value is above or below the mean.

5.21 The normal table provides the areas under the standard normal curve (the distribution of the z values).

5.23 a. $z = \dfrac{25-30}{5} = -1$; x is one standard deviation below the mean.

b. $z = \dfrac{15-30}{5} = -3$; x is three standard deviations below the mean.

c. $z = \dfrac{30-30}{5} = 0$; x is equal to the mean.

d. $z = \dfrac{40-30}{5} = 2$; x is two standard deviations above the mean.

e. $z = \dfrac{50-30}{5} = 4$; x is four standard deviations above the mean.

5.25 a. $z_{.01} = 2.33$

b. $z_{.05} = 1.645$

c. $z_{.02} = 2.054$ or 2.05 with rounding

d. $-z_{.01} = -2.33$

e. $-z_{.05} = -1.645$

f. $-z_{.10} = -1.28$

5.27 First find the z-value from the table that makes the statement true. Then calculate x using the formula:

$x = z\sigma + \mu = z(100) + 500$

    a. $P(x \geq 696) = .025$

    b. $P(x \geq 664.5) = .05$

    c. $P(x < 304) = .025$

    d. $P(x \leq 283) = .015$

    e. $P(x < 717) = .985$

    f. $P(x > 335.5) = .95$

    g. $P(x \leq 696) = .975$

    h. $P(x \geq 700) = .0228$

    i. $P(x > 300) = .9772$

5.29   **a.**   (1) $P(x \leq 959) = P(z \leq 2.12) = .5 + .4830 = .9830$ OR
             Using Cum. Normal Table $P(z \leq 2.12) = .9830$
             (2) $P(x > 1004) = P(z > 2.72) = .5 - .4967 = .0033$ OR
             Using Cum. Normal Table $P(z > 2.72) = 1 - .9967 = .0033$
             (3) $P(x < 650) + P(x > 950) = P(z < -2) + P(z > 2) = 2(.0228) = .0456$ OR
             Using Cum. Normal Table $P(z < -2) + P(z > 2) = .0228 + (1 - .9772) = .0456$

    b. $P(x > 947) = P(z > 1.96) = .025$

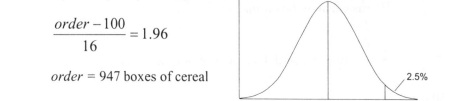

         $\dfrac{order - 100}{16} = 1.96$

         $order = 947$ boxes of cereal

5.31   **a.** $P(x \leq 27) = P(z \leq -3.00) = .5 - .4987 = .0013$ OR

         Using the Cum. Normal table $P(z \leq -3.00) = .0013$

    b.   Claim is probably not true, because the probability is very low of randomly purchasing a car with 27 mpg if the mean is actually 30 mpg.

5.33 $P(x < 15.95) + P(x > 16.05) = P\left(z < \dfrac{15.95 - 16.0024}{.02454} \right) + P\left(z > \dfrac{16.05 - 16.0024}{.02454} \right)$
                          $= P(z < -2.14) + P(z > 1.94) = .0162 + .0262 = .0424$

     Using the cum. normal table $P(z < -2.14) + P(z > 1.94) = .0162 + (1 - .9738) = .0424$

5.35   **a.**   10%, 90%

$$z = \frac{k - \mu}{\sigma}$$

$$-1.28 = \frac{k - 12.4}{20.6}$$

$$k = -13.968$$

      b. $Q_1:$ $-0.67 = \dfrac{k - 12.4}{20.6}$

             $k = -1.402$

           $Q_3:$ $0.67 = \dfrac{k - 12.4}{20.6}$

             $k = 26.202$

5.37   **a.** $[\mu \pm 2.33\sigma]$

      b. $[50.575 \pm 2.33(1.6438)] = [46.745, 54.405]$

5.39   **a.**   Process A: $P(x > 2500) = P\left(z > \dfrac{2500 - 0}{5000}\right) = P(z > .5) = .5 - .1915 = .3085$

            Using the cum. normal table $P(z > .5) = 1 - .6915 = .3085$

            Process B: $P(x > 2500) = P\left(z > \dfrac{2500 - 0}{10,000}\right) = P(z > .25) = .5 - .0987 = .4013$

            Using the cum. normal table $P(z > .25) = 1 - .5987 = .4013$

            Process B is investigated more often.

      b.   Process A: $P(x > 2500) = P\left(z > \dfrac{2500 - 7500}{5000}\right) = P(z > -1) = .5 + .3413 = .8413$

            Using the cum. normal table $P(z > -1) = 1 - .1587 = .8413$

            Process B: $P(x > 2500) = P\left(z > \dfrac{2500 - 7500}{10,000}\right) = P(z > -.5) = .5 + .1915 = .6915$

            Using the cum. normal table $P(z > -.5) = 1 - .3085 = .6915$

            Process A is investigated more often.

      c.   Process B will be investigated more often.

d. $P(x > k) = .3085$ implies that $z = \dfrac{k-0}{10,000} = .5$. Thus $k = 5000$.

Investigate if cost variance exceeds $5000.

$$P(x > 5000) = P\left(z > \frac{5000 - 7500}{10,000}\right) = P(z > -.25) = .5 + .0987 = .5987$$

Using the cum. normal table $P(z > -.25) = 1 - .4013 = .5987$

5.41 $\dfrac{656 - \mu}{\sigma} = -.44 \qquad \dfrac{896 - \mu}{\sigma} = 1.96$

$656 - \mu = -.44\sigma \qquad 896 - \mu = 1.96\sigma$

$-\mu = -.44\sigma - 656 \qquad -\mu = 1.96\sigma - 896$

$\mu = .44\sigma + 656 \qquad \mu = -1.96\sigma + 896$

$.44\sigma + 656 = -1.96\sigma + 896$

$2.4\sigma = 896 - 656$

$2.4\sigma = 240$

$\sigma = 100$

$\mu = .44\sigma + 646$

$\mu = .44(100) + 656 = 44 + 656 = 700$

5.43 Both np and $n(1 - p)$ exceed 5.

5.45 **a.** $np = (200)(.4) = 80$

$n(1 - p) = (200)(.6) = 120$

both ≥ 5

b. $\mu = np = (200)(.4) = 80, \sigma = \sqrt{npq} = \sqrt{48} = 6.9282$ Rounding z to 2 decimal places

(1) $P(x = 80) = P(79.5 \leq x \leq 80.5) = P(-.072 \leq x \leq .072) = .0576$ .0558

(2) $P(x \leq 95) = P(x \leq 95.5) = P(z \leq 2.237) = .9874$ .9875

(3) $P(x < 65) = P(x \leq 64.5) = P(z \leq -2.237) = .0126$ .0125

(4) $P(x \geq 100) = P(x \geq 99.5) = P(z \geq 2.8146) = .0024$ .0025

(5) $P(x > 100) = P(x \geq 100.5) = P(z \geq 2.959) = .0015$

5.47 **a.** (1) Both np and $n(1 - p)$ exceed 5.

(2) $\mu = np = (1000)(.2) = 200, \sigma = \sqrt{npq} = \sqrt{160} = 12.6491$

(3) $P(x \leq 150) = P(x \leq 150.5) = P(z \leq -3.913) = $ less than .001

b. No. If the claim were true, the probability of observing this survey result is less than .001.

5.49 **a.** $\mu = (250)(.05) = 12.5, \sigma = \sqrt{11.875} = 3.446$

$$P(x \geq 40) = P\left(z \geq \frac{39.5 - 12.5}{3.446}\right) = 0 \text{ (approximately)}$$

b. No

5.51 Explanations will vary.

5.53   Explanations will vary.

5.55   **a.** $f(x) = 3e^{-3x}$ for $x \geq 0$.

b.   Graph not included in this manual.

c. $P(x \leq 1) = .9502$

d. $P(.25 \leq x \leq 1) = .4226$

e. $P(x \geq 2) = .0025$

f. $\mu_x = \dfrac{1}{3}, \sigma_x^2 = \dfrac{1}{9}, \sigma_x = \dfrac{1}{3}$

g. $\left[\mu_x \pm 2\sigma_x\right] = \left[-\dfrac{1}{3}, 1\right], P\left(-\dfrac{1}{3} \leq x \leq 1\right) = .9502$

5.57   **a.** $f(x) = \dfrac{2}{3}e^{-2x/3}$ for $x \geq 0$.

b.   Graph not included in this manual.

c. $P(a \leq x \leq b) = e^{-\lambda a} - e^{-\lambda b} = e^{-2a/3} - e^{-2b/3}$
   (1) $P(x \leq 3) = .8647$
   (2) $P(1 \leq x \leq 2) = .2498$
   (3) $P(x > 4) = .0695$
   (4) $P(x < .5) = .2835$

5.59   **a.** $\lambda = 1$
   (1) $P(x > 2) = e^{-2} = .1353$
   (2) $P(1 \leq x \leq 2) = e^{-1} - e^{-2} = .2325$
   (3) $P(x < .25) = 1 - e^{-.25} = .2212$

b.   Probably not; the probability of this happening is .2212 (which is not terribly small).

5.61   **a.** $1 - P(71 \leq x \leq 76) = 1 - P(\dfrac{71 - 73.5}{1} \leq z \leq \dfrac{76 - 73.5}{1}) = 1 - P(-2.5 \leq z \leq 2.5)$
$= 1 - .9876 = .0124$

b. $P(x \geq 74) = P(z \geq .5) = .5 - .1915 = .3085$

c. $P(x < 70.5) = P(z < -3) = .5 - .4987 = .0013$

5.63 **a.** $f(x) = \dfrac{1}{.5 - (-.5)} = \dfrac{1}{.5 + .5} = 1 \quad for -.5 \le x \le .5$

b.

f(x)

1

  −.5   .5 cents

c. $P(\{x > .3\} \text{ or } \{x < -.3\}) = .2 + .2 = .4$

d. $P(\{x > .1\} \text{ or } \{x < = .1\}) = .4 + .4 = .8$

e. $u_x = \dfrac{c+d}{2} = \dfrac{-.5+.5}{2} = 0$

$\sigma_x = \sqrt{\dfrac{(d-c)^2}{12}} = \sqrt{\dfrac{(.5-(-.5))^2}{12}} = .2887$

f. $[\mu_x \pm \sigma_x] = [0 \pm .2887] = [-.2887, .2887]$
$P(-.2887 \le x \le .2887) = (.2887 - (-.2887))(1) = .5774$

5.65 **a.** 10%, 90%, approximately 3.462

$P(x \le k) = .10$

$z = \dfrac{k - \mu}{\sigma}$

$-1.282 = \dfrac{k-5}{1.2}, \quad k = 3.4616$

Note: if use $z = -1.28$, $k = 3.464$

b. Follow the methods outlined in part a, or compute the inverse cdf in MINITAB.
$Q_1 = 4.196$, $Q_3 = 5.804$

5.67 $P(x < 15) = .004$

$z = \dfrac{15 - \mu}{\sigma}$

$-2.65 = \dfrac{15 - \mu}{.02}$

$\mu = 15.053$
Set to 15.053 inches.

5.69 $\lambda = \dfrac{1}{\mu_x} = \dfrac{4}{1000} = \dfrac{1}{250}$

a. $P(x \ge 400) = e^{-400/250} = .2019$

b. $P(0 \le x \le 100) = e^0 - e^{-100/250} = 1 - .6703 = .3297$

5.71 $P(x > 984,000) = P(z > \dfrac{984,000 - 800,000}{80,000} = P(z > 2.3) = .5 - .4893 = .0107$

5.73 $\mu_x = 60$ sec, $\lambda = 1$

    a. $P(x \geq 1.5\,\text{min}) = e^{-1.5} = .2231$

    b. $P(x \geq 2\,\text{min}) = e^{-2} = .1353$

5.75 $\mu = np = (400)(.50) = 200$

    $\sigma = \sqrt{npq} = \sqrt{(400)(.5)(.5)} = \sqrt{100} = 10$

    a. $P(x \leq 180) = P(z \leq \dfrac{180.5 - 200}{10}) = P(z \leq -1.95) = .5 - .4744 = .0256$

    b. Yes

CHAPTER 6—Sampling Distributions

6.1 Each unit is the mean of four population measurements.

6.3 They are the same.

6.5 If the sample size n is sufficiently large, then the population of all sample means is approximately normal.

6.7 **a.** $\mu_{\bar{x}} = 10$

$$\sigma_{\bar{x}}^2 = \frac{\sigma^2}{n} = \frac{2^2}{25} = \frac{4}{25} = .16$$

$$\sigma_{\bar{x}} = \frac{\sigma}{\sqrt{n}} = \frac{2}{\sqrt{25}} = \frac{2}{5} = .4$$

b. $\mu_{\bar{x}} = 500$

$$\sigma_{\bar{x}}^2 = \frac{\sigma^2}{n} = \frac{(.5)^2}{100} = \frac{.25}{100} = .0025$$

$$\sigma_{\bar{x}} = \frac{\sigma}{\sqrt{n}} = \frac{.5}{\sqrt{100}} = \frac{.5}{10} = .05$$

c. $\mu_{\bar{x}} = 3$

$$\sigma_{\bar{x}}^2 = \frac{\sigma^2}{n} = \frac{(.1)^2}{4} = \frac{.01}{4} = .0025$$

$$\sigma_{\bar{x}} = \frac{\sigma}{\sqrt{n}} = \frac{.1}{\sqrt{4}} = \frac{.1}{2} = .05$$

d. $\mu_{\bar{x}} = 100$

$$\sigma_{\bar{x}}^2 = \frac{\sigma^2}{n} = \frac{(1)^2}{1600} = \frac{1}{1600} = .000625$$

$$\sigma_{\bar{x}} = \frac{\sigma}{\sqrt{n}} = \frac{1}{\sqrt{1600}} = \frac{1}{40} = .025$$

6.9 **a.** Normally distributed; no, because the sample size is large (≥ 30)

b. $\mu_{\bar{x}} = 20, \sigma_{\bar{x}} = \frac{\sigma}{\sqrt{n}} = \frac{4}{\sqrt{64}} = \frac{4}{8} = .5$

c. $P(\bar{x} > 21) = P\left(z > \frac{21 - 20}{.5}\right) = P(z > 2) = .5 - .4772 = .0228$

d. $P(\bar{x} < 19.385) = P\left(z < \frac{19.385 - 20}{.5}\right) = P(z < -1.23) = .5 - .3907 = .1093$

6.11 **a.** Normal because the sample is large ($n \geq 30$)

b. $\mu_{\bar{x}} = 6, \sigma_{\bar{x}} = \dfrac{\sigma}{\sqrt{n}} = \dfrac{2.47}{\sqrt{100}} = .247$

c. $P(\bar{x} \leq 5.46) = P\left(z \leq \dfrac{5.46 - 6}{.247} \right) = P(z \leq -2.19) = .5 - .4857 = .0143$

d. 1.43%; conclude that μ is less than 6.

6.13 **a.** $\mu_{\bar{x}} = \mu = 1.4$

$\sigma_{\bar{x}} = \dfrac{\sigma}{\sqrt{n}} = \dfrac{1.3}{\sqrt{100}} = \dfrac{1.3}{10} = .13$

$P(\bar{x} > 1.5) = P\left(z > \dfrac{1.5 - 1.4}{.13} \right) = P(z > .77) = .5 - .2794 = .2206$

b. $\mu_{\bar{x}} = \mu = 1.0$

$\sigma_{\bar{x}} = \dfrac{\sigma}{\sqrt{n}} = \dfrac{1.8}{\sqrt{100}} = \dfrac{1.8}{10} = .18$

$P(\bar{x} > 1.5) = P\left(z > \dfrac{1.5 - 1.0}{.18} \right) = P(z > 2.78) = .5 - .4973 = .0027$

c. Yes, the probability of observing the sample is very small if the mean is actually 1.0.

6.15 Population of all possible sample proportions ($\hat{p}$ *values*)

6.17 Decreases the spread of all possible $\hat{p}$ values.

6.19 **a.** $\mu_{\hat{p}} = p = .5$

$\sigma_{\hat{p}}^2 = \dfrac{p(1-p)}{n} = \dfrac{.5(1-.5)}{250} = \dfrac{.25}{250} = .001$

$\sigma_{\hat{p}} = \sqrt{\dfrac{p(1-p)}{n}} = \sqrt{.001} = .0316$

b. $\mu_{\hat{p}} = p = .1$

$\sigma_{\hat{p}}^2 = \dfrac{p(1-p)}{n} = \dfrac{.1(.9)}{100} = .0009$

$\sigma_{\hat{p}} = \sqrt{\dfrac{p(1-p)}{n}} = .03$

c. $\mu_{\hat{p}} = p = .8$

$\sigma_{\hat{p}}^2 = \dfrac{p(1-p)}{n} = \dfrac{.8(.2)}{400} = .0004$

$\sigma_{\hat{p}} = \sqrt{\dfrac{p(1-p)}{n}} = .02$

d. $\mu_{\hat{p}} = p = .98$

$$\sigma_{\hat{p}}^2 = \frac{p(1-p)}{n} = \frac{.98(1-.98)}{1000} = .0000196$$

$$\sigma_{\hat{p}} = \sqrt{\frac{p(1-p)}{n}} = .004427$$

6.21 a. $np = (100)(.9) = 90 : n(1-p) = (100)(.1) = 10 :$ The sample is large enough

The distribution of $\hat{p}$ is normally distributed.

b. $\mu_{\hat{p}} = p = .9$

$$\sigma_{\hat{p}} = \sqrt{\frac{p(1-p)}{n}} = \sqrt{\frac{.9(1-.9)}{100}} = .03$$

c. (1) $P(\hat{p} \geq .96) = P\left(z \geq \frac{.96 - .9}{.03}\right) = P(z \geq 2) = .5 - .4772 = .0228$

(2) $P(.855 \leq \hat{p} \leq .945) = P\left(\frac{.855 - .9}{.03} \leq \hat{p} \leq \frac{.945 - .9}{.03}\right) = P(-1.5 \leq z \leq 1.5) = 2(.4332) = .8664$

(3) $P(\hat{p} \leq .915) = P\left(z \leq \frac{.915 - .9}{.03}\right) = P(z \leq .5) = .5 + .1915 = .6915$

6.23 a. $\mu_{\hat{p}} = p = .30$

$$\sigma_{\hat{p}} = \sqrt{\frac{(.30)(1-.30)}{1011}} = .0144$$

$$P(\hat{p} \geq .32) = P(z \geq \frac{.32 - .30}{.0144}) = P(z \geq 1.39) = .5 - .4177 = .0823$$

b. Perhaps, evidence not very strong.

6.25 a. (1) $P(.45 \leq \hat{p} \leq .51) = P\left(\frac{.45 - .48}{.0267} \leq z \leq \frac{.51 - .48}{.0267}\right) = P(-1.12 \leq z \leq 1.12) = 0.7372$

(2) $P(.42 \leq \hat{p} \leq .54) = P\left(\frac{.42 - .48}{.0267} \leq z \leq \frac{.54 - .48}{.0267}\right) = P(-2.25 \leq z \leq 2.25) = 0.9756$

b. Closer to $\pm 6\%$ because margin of error is usually at 95% probability.

6.27a. $\mu_{\hat{p}} = p = .20$

$$\sigma_{\hat{p}} = \sqrt{\frac{(.20)(.80)}{1000}} = .0126$$

$$P(\hat{p} \le .15) = P(z \le \frac{.15 - .20}{.0126}) = P(z \le -3.97)$$

$$= \text{less than } .001$$

b. Yes, the probability of observing this sample is very small if $p = .20$. The true p is probably less than .20.

6.29 $\mu = 2000, \sigma = 300$

a. $P(x > 2150) = P\left(z > \frac{2150 - 2000}{300}\right) = P(z > .5) = .5 - .1915 = .3085$

b. $\mu_{\bar{x}} = 2000, \sigma_{\bar{x}} = \frac{\sigma}{\sqrt{n}} = \frac{300}{\sqrt{36}} = 50$

$$P(\bar{x} > 2150) = P\left(z > \frac{2150 - 2000}{50}\right) = P(z > 3) = .5 - .4987 = .0013$$

c. More difficult to achieve an average that exceeds $2150; yes

d. Explanations will vary.

6.31 **a.** $\mu_{\hat{p}} = p = .25$

$$\sigma_{\hat{p}} = \sqrt{\frac{(.25)(.75)}{757}} = 0.0157$$

$$P(\hat{p} \ge .297) = P(z \ge \frac{.297 - .25}{.0157}) = P(z \ge 2.99) = 0.0014$$

b. Yes, the probability that $p \ge .297$ is very small.

6.33 **a.** $\mu_{\bar{x}} = \mu = 50$

$$\sigma_{\bar{x}} = \frac{\sigma}{\sqrt{n}} = \frac{.6}{\sqrt{100}} = \frac{.6}{10} = .06$$

$$P(49.88 \le \bar{x} \le 50.12) = P\left(\frac{49.88 - 50}{.06} \le z \le \frac{50.12 - 50}{.06}\right) = P(-2 < z < 2)$$

$$= 2(.4772) = .9544$$

b. $P(\bar{x} < 49.85) = P\left(z < \frac{49.85 - 50}{.06}\right) = P(z < -2.5) = .5 - .4938 = .0062$

6.35 **a.** $P(\hat{p} \le .41) = P\left(z \le \frac{.41 - .5}{.01414}\right) = P(z \le -6.36);$ less than .001.

b. Yes, conclude $p < .5$.

6.37 **a.** $\mu_{\bar{x}} = 50.6, \sigma_{\bar{x}} = \dfrac{\sigma}{\sqrt{n}} = \dfrac{1.62}{\sqrt{5}} = .7245$

$[50.6 \pm 2(.7245)] = [49.151, 52.049]$

b. $\mu_{\bar{x}} = 50.6, \sigma_{\bar{x}} = \dfrac{\sigma}{\sqrt{n}} = \dfrac{1.62}{\sqrt{40}} = .256$

$[50.6 \pm 2(.256)] = [50.088, 51.112]$

c. $n = 40$, A sample of 40 results in a more accurate estimate of μ

6.39 **a.** $\mu_{\hat{p}} = p = .50$

$\sigma_{\hat{p}} = \sqrt{\dfrac{(.50)(.50)}{622}} = .020$

$P(\hat{p} \geq .59) = P(z \geq \dfrac{.59 - .50}{.020}) = P(z \geq 4.5) = \text{less than } .001$

b. Yes, the probability of observing this sample is extremely small if $p = .50$. More likely the true p is greater than .50.

6.41 **a.** $\mu_{\bar{x}} = 500$

$\sigma_{\bar{x}} = \dfrac{40}{\sqrt{35}} = 6.76$

$P(\bar{x} \geq 538) = P(z \geq \dfrac{538 - 500}{6.76}) = P(z \geq 5.62) = \text{less than } .0001$

b. Yes, the probability of this sample is extremely small if $\mu = \$500$. The mean is more likely greater than $500.

Internet Exercises

6.43   Screen from CLT module:

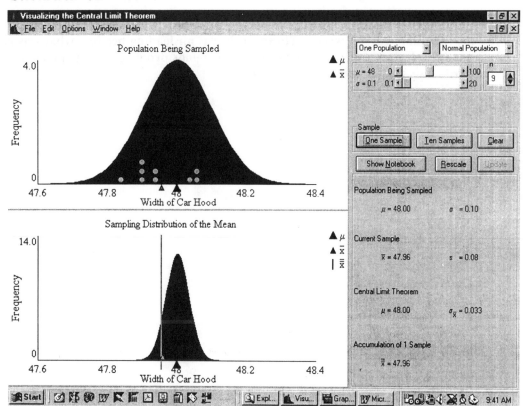

Exercises:

Sampling a Normal Population

Press the Show Notebook button, select the Scenarios tab, click on Normal Distribution, and select Width of Car Hood. Read the scenario and click on OK.

1.   What is the mean and standard deviation of the population being sampled? What is the mean and standard error of the sampling distribution? What is the relationship between the standard deviation of the population being sampled and the sampling distribution? If you aren't sure use the Help option on the menu bar.

Population Being Sampled: Mean _____**48**_____   Standard Deviation _____**0.1**_____

Sampling Distribution: Mean _____**48**_____   Standard Error _____**0.033**_____

Standard Error = Standard Deviation / $\sqrt{\textbf{Sample Size}}$

3. Was the salesman wrong when he said that his company's machine has a standard error of 0.033? Why was his statement misleading?

   No, the salesman was not wrong. However, it was misleading because what was relevant was the standard deviation of the distribution of car hoods produced by the machine, not the standard error of the sampling distribution.

CHAPTER 7—Confidence Intervals

7.1 There is an entire population of possible sample means. A confidence interval is constructed to be confident that the true value of μ is contained in that interval.

7.3 The higher the confidence level, the wider the confidence interval. The larger the sample, the shorter the confidence interval.

  a. longer

  b. shorter

  c. shorter

  d. longer

7.5 $\left[\bar{x} \pm z_{\alpha/2} \dfrac{\sigma}{\sqrt{n}} \right]$

  a. $\left[50 \pm (1.96)\left(\dfrac{2}{\sqrt{100}} \right) \right] = [49.608, 50.392]$

  b. $\left[50 \pm (2.575)\left(\dfrac{2}{\sqrt{100}} \right) \right] = [49.485, 50.515]$

  c. $\left[50 \pm (2.17)\left(\dfrac{2}{\sqrt{100}} \right) \right] = [49.566, 50.434]$

  d. $\left[50 \pm (1.28)\left(\dfrac{2}{\sqrt{100}} \right) \right] = [49.744, 50.256]$

  e. $\left[50 \pm 3\left(\dfrac{2}{\sqrt{100}} \right) \right] = [49.400, 50.600]$

7.7 **a.** $\left[5.46 \pm 1.96\left(\dfrac{2.47}{\sqrt{100}} \right) \right] = [4.976, 5.944]$

  $\left[5.46 \pm 2.575\left(\dfrac{2.47}{\sqrt{100}} \right) \right] = [4.824, 6.096]$

  b. Yes, 95% interval is below 6.

  c. No, 99% interval extends above 6.

  d. Fairly confident since 95% CI is below 6 while 99% CI contains 6.

7.9　　a.　$\left[5.68 \pm 2.33\left(\dfrac{8.70}{\sqrt{100}}\right)\right] = [3.653, 7.707]$

　　　　b.　3.653

7.11　a.　$\left[82.6 \pm 1.96\left(\dfrac{33}{\sqrt{100}}\right)\right] = [76.132, 89.068]$

　　　　b.　$\left[93 \pm 1.96\left(\dfrac{37}{\sqrt{100}}\right)\right] = [85.748, 100.252]$

　　　　c.　Mean audit delay for public owner controlled companies appears to be shorter, since there is only a small amount of overlap of the intervals.

7.13　a.　Decreases

　　　　b.　Decreases

7.15　For 11 dfs $t_{.10} = 1.363, t_{.025} = 2.201, t_{.001} = 4.025$

　　　　For 6 dfs $t_{.10} = 1.440, t_{.025} = 2.447, t_{.001} = 5.208$

7.17　a.　$\left[6 \pm 2.447\left(\dfrac{1.8257}{\sqrt{7}}\right)\right] = [4.311, 7.689]$

　　　　　$\left[6 \pm 3.707\left(\dfrac{1.8257}{\sqrt{7}}\right)\right] = [3.442, 8.558]$

　　　　b.　Can be 95% confident the claim is true. Cannot be 99% confident the claim is true.

7.19　a.　$\left[13.8 \pm 2.093\left(\dfrac{1.57}{\sqrt{20}}\right)\right] = [13.065, 14.535]$

　　　　b.　Yes, 95% interval is below 17.

7.21　a.　$\left[811 \pm 2.776\left(\dfrac{19.6469}{\sqrt{5}}\right)\right] = [786.609, 835.391]$

　　　　b.　Yes, the 95% interval is above 750.

7.23　t-based 95% CI: [4.969, 5.951]
　　　　Minitab: [4.9688, 5.9512]
　　　　Yes, interval is less than 6.

7.25　The margin of error refers to the error of our sample mean as an estimate of the population mean, due to sampling variability.

7.27　Because σ is unknown and must be estimated by s obtained from a preliminary sample.

7.29 **a.** $n = \left(\dfrac{1.984(32.83)}{4}\right)^2 = 266$ companies

b. $n = \left(\dfrac{2.626(32.83)}{4}\right)^2 = 465$ companies

7.31 **a.** $n = \left(\dfrac{2.776(19.65)}{8}\right)^2 = 47$ trial runs

b. $n = \left(\dfrac{4.604(19.65)}{5}\right)^2 = 328$ trial runs

7.33 $n = \left(\dfrac{2.093(1.57)}{.5}\right)^2 = 44$ stabilization times

7.35 **a.** $p = .5$

b. $p = .3$

c. $p = .8$

7.37 95% C.I.: $z_{\alpha/2} = 1.96$
98% C.I.: $z_{\alpha/2} = 2.33$
99% C.I.: $z_{\alpha/2} = 2.575$

a. $\left[.4 \pm z_{\alpha/2}\sqrt{\dfrac{(.4)(.6)}{100}}\right]$; [.304, .496], [.286, .514], [.274, .526]

b. $\left[.1 \pm z_{\alpha/2}\sqrt{\dfrac{(.1)(.9)}{300}}\right]$; [.066, .134], [.060, .140], [.055, .145]

c. $\left[.9 \pm z_{\alpha/2}\sqrt{\dfrac{(.9)(.1)}{100}}\right]$; [.841, .959], [.830, .970], [.823, .977]

d. $\left[.6 \pm z_{\alpha/2}\sqrt{\dfrac{(.6)(.4)}{50}}\right]$; [.464, .736], [.439, .761], [.422, .778]

7.39 **a.** $\left[.54146 \pm 1.96\sqrt{\dfrac{(.54146)(.45854)}{205}}\right] = [.473, .610]$

b. No, the interval extends below .5.

7.41 **a.** $.42 \pm 2.575 \sqrt{\dfrac{(.42)(.58)}{1031}} = .42 \pm .04 = [.3804, .4596]$

No

b. $.60 \pm 1.96 \sqrt{\dfrac{(.60)(.40)}{1031}} = .60 \pm .03 = [.5701, .6299]$

Yes

c. 95% margin of error is .03

7.43 **a.** $\left[.67 \pm 2.575 \sqrt{\dfrac{(.67)(.33)}{418}}\right] = [.611, .729]$

b. Yes, the interval is above .6.

7.45 $\hat{p} = \dfrac{512}{500} = 0.304$

a. $\left[.304 \pm 1.96 \sqrt{\dfrac{(.304)(.696)}{500}}\right] = [.264, .344]$

b. Yes, the interval is above 0.20.

7.47 **a.** $\hat{p} = \dfrac{10}{500} = .02$

$\left[.02 \pm 1.96 \sqrt{\dfrac{(.02)(.98)}{500}}\right] = [.0077, .0323]$

b. $\hat{p} = \dfrac{27}{500} = .054$

$\left[.054 \pm 1.96 \sqrt{\dfrac{(.054)(.946)}{500}}\right] = [.034, .074]$

c. Yes, the confidence interval is higher.

7.49 Using p = .73754 and $z_{.005} = 2.576$

$n = .73754\,(1 - .73754)\left(\dfrac{2.576}{.03}\right)^{2}$

$= 1429.13$ so

n = 1430

7.51 A tolerance interval is supposed to contain a specified percentage of individual population measurements.

7.53   The tolerance interval contains individual measurements which includes the high and low measurements that are averaged out in the confidence interval of the mean.

7.55   68.26% tolerance interval: $5.46 \pm 2.475 = [2.985, 7.935]$

95.44% tolerance interval: $5.46 \pm 4.95 = [0.51, 10.41]$

99.73% tolerance interval: $5.46 \pm 7.425 = [-1.965, 12.885]$

95% confidence interval: $5.46 \pm 1.984(2.475/\sqrt{100}) = [4.9690, 5.9510]$

7.57   **a.** $\left[68.04 \pm 1.97\left(\dfrac{35.72}{\sqrt{250}}\right)\right] = [63.590, 72.490]$

b. $\left[56.74 \pm 1.97\left(\dfrac{34.87}{\sqrt{238}}\right)\right] = [52.287, 61.93]$

c.   Yes, interval is below the lowest value in the confidence interval.

7.59   **a.** $.61 \pm 1.96\sqrt{\dfrac{(.61)(.39)}{622}} = .61 \pm .038 = [.572, .648]$

Yes

b.   95% margin of error is .038

7.61   **a.** $57.8 \pm 1.993\left(\dfrac{6.02}{\sqrt{81}}\right) = [56.467, 59.133]$

Yes, interval is below 60.

b. $n = \left(\dfrac{Z_{\alpha/2}s}{B}\right)^2 = \left[\dfrac{1.993(6.02)}{1}\right]^2 = 143.95 \approx 144$

7.63   **a.** $\left[26.22 \pm 2.01\left(\dfrac{3.7432}{\sqrt{50}}\right)\right] = [25.1562, 27.2838]$

b.   Yes, not much more than 25

7.65   **a.** $95\% \ C.I. = \left[\bar{x} \pm 2.01\dfrac{s}{\sqrt{n}}\right]$

Fixed annuities: [7.685%, 7.975%]
Domestic large-cap stocks: [9.108%, 17.732%]
Domestic mid-cap stocks: [9.788%, 20.272%]
Domestic small-cap stocks: [16.327%, 28.693%]

      b.   Fixed annuities: differ from 8.31%

              Domestic large-cap stocks: does not differ from 11.71%

              Domestic mid-cap stocks: does not differ from 13.64%

              Domestic small-cap stocks: differs from 14.93%

7.67 $\quad .64 \pm 1.96 \sqrt{\dfrac{(.64)(.36)}{1000}} = .64 \pm .02975 = [.61025, .66975]$

7.69   **a.** $\hat{p} = \dfrac{512}{620} = .826 \qquad .826 \pm 2\sqrt{\dfrac{(.826)(.174)}{620}} = [.796, .856]$

      b.   Yes, interval is above .75.

CHAPTER 8—Hypothesis Testing

8.1 H_0 is the status quo hypothesis. H_a says the hoped for (suspected) condition exists.

8.3   **a.**   Type I error: reject H_0 when H_0 is true

      b.   Type II error: do not reject H_0 when H_0 is false

      c. α = probability of a Type I error

      d. β = probability of a Type II error

8.5   Type I error

8.7   Because the probability of a Type II error might become large.

8.9   **a.** $H_0 : \mu \geq 6$ versus $H_a : \mu < 6$.

      b.   Type I: decide $\mu < 6$ when μ is really ≥ 6
           Type II: decide $\mu \geq 6$ when μ is really < 6

8.11   **a.** $H_0 : \mu = 16$ versus $H_a : \mu \neq 16$.

      b.   Type I: decide $\mu \neq 16$ (readjust filler) when $\mu = 16$ (no adjustment is needed)
           Type II: decide $\mu = 16$ (do not readjust) when $\mu \neq 16$ (readjustment may be needed)

8.13   There is a .05 probability that the network will advertise the ZX-900 achieves a shorter mean stopping distance than its competitor when it really does not.

8.15   A p-value is the probability that we obtain a sample statistic that contradicts the null hypothesis as much as or more than the observed sample statistic.

Exercises 8.17 – 8.21 Testing $H_0 : \mu = 80$ versus $H_a : \mu > 80$

8.17
$\alpha = .10$
$z_{.10} = 1.28$

Since 2.5 > 1.28, Reject H_0 with $\alpha = .10$.

8.19
$\alpha = .01$
$z_{.01} = 2.33$

Since 2.5 > 2.33, Reject H_0 with $\alpha = .01$.

8.21 $z = 2.5$
p-value = .5 – .4938 = .0062
Since .0062 is less than .10, .05, and .01 but not less than .001, reject H_0 at $\alpha = $ .10, .05, .01, but not at $\alpha = $ .001.

Exercises 8.23 – 8.29 Testing $H_0 : \mu = 20$ versus $H_a : \mu < 20$

8.23 $z = \dfrac{18 - 20}{7 / \sqrt{49}} = -2$

8.25 $\alpha = .05$

$-z_{.05} = -1.645$

Since $-2 < -1.645$, Reject H_0 with $\alpha = .05$.

8.27 $\alpha = .001$

$-z_{.001} = -3.09$

Since -2 is not less than -3.09 cannot reject H_0 with $\alpha = .001$.

8.29 Since *p*-value = .0228 is less than .05, there is strong evidence.

8.31 $H_0 : \mu \geq 6$ versus $H_a : \mu < 6$.

  a. $z = -2.19$

   Rejection points

$$-z_{.10} = -1.28$$
$$-z_{.05} = -1.645$$
$$-z_{.01} = -2.33$$
$$-z_{.001} = -3.09$$

   Since -2.19 is less than -1.28 and -1.645, reject H_0 with $\alpha = .10$ and .05, but not with $\alpha = .01$ and .001.

  b. *p*-value $= .5 - .4857 = .0143$

   Since *p*-value$=.0143$ is less than .10 and .05, reject H_0 at those levels of α, but not with $\alpha = .01$ or .001.

  c. There is strong evidence.

8.33 $H_0 : \mu \leq 31$ versus $H_a : \mu > 31$.

$$z = \dfrac{31.5531 - 31}{\dfrac{.8}{\sqrt{49}}} = 4.84$$

$z_{.05} = 1.645$

Since $4.84 > 1.645$, reject H_0 at $\alpha = .05$. Award the tax credit.

p-value = less than .001, This is less than .01 so   reject H_0 at $\alpha = .01$. There is extremely strong evidence against H_0 .

8.35 $H_0 : \mu \geq 60$ versus $H_a : \mu < 60$.

$\bar{x} = 57.8, \sigma = 6.02, z = -3.29$, so reject H_0 , run the commercial.

95% CI: $57.8 \pm (1.96) \dfrac{6.02}{\sqrt{81}} = [56.489, 59.111]$

There might be some practical importance, because μ might be enough (less than 60) to prevent some accidents.

8.37   See page 322, answers will vary. Statistical significance relates to variability while practical importance relates to some context specific definitions for what makes for a practical important difference.

Exercises 8.39 – 8.43 Testing $H_0 : \mu = 40$ **versus** $H_a : \mu \neq 40$

8.39 $\alpha = .10$

$z_{.10/2} = 1.645$

Since $|-3| > 1.645$, Reject H_0 with $\alpha = .10$.

8.41 $\alpha = .01$

$z_{.01/2} = 2.575$

Since $|-3| > 2.575$, reject H_0 with $\alpha = .01$.

8.43 $z = -3$
p-value $= 2(.5 - .4987) = .0026$
Since .0026 is less than .10, .05 and .01, but not less than .001, reject H_0 at $\alpha = .10, .05$, and .01, but not at $\alpha = .001$.

8.45   **a.** $H_0 : \mu = 3$ versus $H_a : \mu \neq 3$.

$z = \dfrac{3.006 - 3}{\dfrac{.016}{\sqrt{40}}} = 2.37$

$z_{\alpha/2} = z_{.025} = 1.96$, Since $2.37 > 1.96$, reject H_0 with $\alpha = .05$.

p-value $= 2(.5 - .4911) = .0178$, Since p-value$=.0178$ is less than .05, reject H_0 with $\alpha = .05$.

The problem-solving team should be assigned.

b. $[\bar{x} \pm 3\sigma] = [3.006 \pm 3(.016)] = [2.958, 3.054]$

Some diameters will exceed the upper specification limit of 3.05 inches.

8.47 $n=36$, $\bar{x} = 16.05$, $\sigma = .1$

$$95\% \text{ C.I. } \left[\bar{x} \pm z_{\alpha/2} \frac{\sigma}{\sqrt{n}} \right] = \left[16.05 \pm 1.96 \frac{.1}{\sqrt{36}} \right] = \left[16.0173, 16.0827 \right]$$

Since $\mu = 16$ does not fall within the 95% C.I., reject H_0 with $\alpha = .05$.

Considerations for practical importance might be production volume, cost per ounce, etc.

8.49   Small sample ($n < 30$), unknown σ, normal population.

8.51   **a.** $t = \dfrac{\bar{x} - \mu_0}{\dfrac{s}{\sqrt{n}}} = \dfrac{13.5 - 10}{\dfrac{6}{\sqrt{16}}} = 2.33$

  15 degrees of freedom

  $t_{.10} = 1.341$; reject H_0 at $\alpha = .10$.

  $t_{.05} = 1.753$; reject H_0 at $\alpha = .05$

  $t_{.01} = 2.602$; do not reject H_0 at $\alpha = .01$.

  $t_{.001} = 3.733$; do not reject H_0 at $\alpha = .001$.

8.53   **a.** $H_0 : \mu \le 3.5\%$ versus $H_a : \mu > 3.5\%$.

  b. $\bar{x} = 6, s = 1.826, n = 7$, degrees of freedom $= 6$, $\mu_0 = 3.5$

  $t = \dfrac{6 - 3.5}{\dfrac{1.826}{\sqrt{7}}} = 3.62$

  $t_{.01} = 3.143, t_{.001} = 5.208$

  Since $3.143 < 3.62 < 5.208$, reject $H_0 : \mu \le 3.5\%$ at $\alpha = .10, .05, .01$, but not at $\alpha = .001$. There is very strong evidence that H_0 is false.

  c.   Explanations will vary.

8.55   **a.** $H_0 : \mu \le 50$ versus $H_a : \mu > 50$

  b. $t = \dfrac{54 - 50}{\dfrac{8}{\sqrt{25}}} = 2.5$

  24 degrees of freedom, $t_{.01} = 2.492, t_{.001} = 3.467$

  Since $2.492 < 2.5 < 3.467$, reject H_0 at $\alpha = .10, .05, .01$, but not at $\alpha = .001$. There is very strong evidence that H_0 is false.

  c.   Explanations will vary.

8.57   *p*-value = .002261 so reject H_0 at α = .1, .05, and .01 and do not reject at α = .001. Very strong evidence.

8.59   Yes, because $46 per square foot represents an important increase in sales.

8.61 $H_0 : \mu \geq 6, \quad H_A : \mu < 6$

$$t = \frac{5.46 - 6}{2.475/\sqrt{100}} = -2.18$$

$-t_{.05} = -1.660$ so reject H_0.

The *p*-value of .0158 means we would reject H_0 at .1 and .05 but do not reject at α = .01 and .001.

8.63   *p* is the true proportion of all voters who prefer a political candidate, where $\hat{p}$ is the fraction of the sample who prefer a political candidate.

8.65   *p* is the true proportion of all units that are defective, where $\hat{p}$ is the fraction of the sample that are defective.

8.67 $[np, \; n(1-p)]$

   a.   [200, 200]; yes, large enough

   b.   [1, 99]; no, not large enough

   c.   [100, 9900]; yes

   d.   [20, 80]; yes

   e.   [179.2, 76.8]; yes

   f.   [196, 4]; no

   g.   [980, 20], yes

   h.   [10, 15]; yes

8.69 $H_0 : p = .3$ versus $H_a : p \neq .3$.

   a. $$z = \frac{.2 - .3}{\sqrt{\dfrac{.3(.7)}{100}}} = -2.18$$

   $-z_{.01/2} = -z_{.005} = -2.575$
   Since $-2.575 < -2.18$, do not reject H_0.

   b.   *p*-value = $2P(z > 2.18) = .0292$

   c.   Reject H_0 at α = .10 and .05, but not at α = .01 or .001.

8.71 **a.** $H_0 : p \le .5$ versus $H_a : p > .50$.

b. $\hat{p} = \dfrac{111}{205} = .5415$

$z = \dfrac{.5415 - .5}{\sqrt{\dfrac{(.5)^2}{205}}} = 1.19$

$z_{.10} = 1.28$

Since $1.19 < 1.28$, do not reject H_0 for any of the α-values; little evidence.

c. $\hat{p} = \dfrac{540}{1000} = .54$

$z = \dfrac{.54 - .5}{\sqrt{\dfrac{(.5)^2}{1000}}} = 2.53$

$z_{.01} = 2.33, z_{.001} = 3.09$

Since $2.33 < 2.53 < 3.09$, reject H_0 at $\alpha = .01$, but not at $\alpha = .001$; very strong evidence.

d. $\hat{p} = .54$ based on a much larger sample provides stronger evidence that p is greater than .50.

8.73 **a.** $H_0 : p \le .18$ versus $H_a : p > .18$.

b. $\hat{p} = \dfrac{46}{200} = .23$

$z = \dfrac{.23 - .18}{\sqrt{\dfrac{(.18)(.82)}{200}}} = 1.84$

p-value $= P(z > 1.84) = .0329$

Reject H_0 at $\alpha = .10$ and $.05$, but not at $\alpha = .01$ or $.001$; strong evidence

c. Perhaps, but this is subjective.

8.75 **a.** $H_0 : p = .95$ versus $H_a : p < .95$.

b. $\hat{p} = \dfrac{316}{400} = .79$

$z = \dfrac{.79 - .95}{\sqrt{\dfrac{.95(.05)}{400}}} = -14.68$

Reject H_0 at each value of α; extremely strong evidence.

c. Probably, $\hat{p} = .79$ is far below the claimed .95.

8.77 The probability of a Type II error varies depending on the alternative value of μ.

8.79 **a.** $H_0 : \mu \le 60$ versus $H_a : \mu > 60$.

$n = 100$, $\sigma = 2$, $\alpha = .025$

Reject H_0 if $z > \dfrac{\bar{x} - 60}{\dfrac{\sigma}{\sqrt{n}}} = \dfrac{\bar{x} - 60}{\dfrac{2}{\sqrt{100}}} = \dfrac{\bar{x} - 60}{.2} > 1.96$

Reject H_0 if $\bar{x} > 60 + .2(1.96) = 60.392$.

Do not reject H_0 if $\bar{x} \le 60.392$.

$\mu = 60.1$

$\beta = P(\bar{x} \le 60.392) = P\left(z \le \dfrac{60.392 - 60.1}{.2} \right) = P\left(z \le \dfrac{.292}{.2} \right) = P(z \le 1.46) = .5 + .4279 = .9279$

$\mu = 60.2$

$\beta = P(\bar{x} \le 60.392) = P\left(z \le \dfrac{60.392 - 60.2}{.2} \right) = P\left(z \le \dfrac{.192}{.2} \right) = P(z \le .96) = .5 + .3315 = .8315$

$\mu = 60.3$

$\beta = P(\bar{x} \le 60.392) = P\left(z \le \dfrac{60.392 - 60.3}{.2} \right) = P\left(z \le \dfrac{.092}{.2} \right) = P(z \le .46) = .5 + .1772 = .6772$

$\mu = 60.4$

$\beta = P(\bar{x} \le 60.392) = P\left(z \le \dfrac{60.392 - 60.4}{.2} \right) = P\left(z \le \dfrac{.008}{.2} \right) = P(z \le -.04) = .5 - .0160$

$= .4840$

$\mu = 60.5$

$\beta = P(\bar{x} \le 60.392) = P\left(z \le \dfrac{60.392 - 60.5}{.2} \right) = P\left(z \le \dfrac{-.108}{.2} \right) = P(z \le -.54) = .5 - .2054$

$= .2946$

$\mu = 60.6$

$\beta = P(\bar{x} \le 60.392) = P\left(z \le \dfrac{60.392 - 60.6}{.2} \right) = P\left(z \le \dfrac{-.208}{.2} \right) = P(z \le 1.04) = .5 - .3508$

$= .1492$

$\mu = 60.7$

$\beta = P(\bar{x} \le 60.392) = P\left(z \le \dfrac{60.392 - 60.7}{.2} \right) = P\left(z \le \dfrac{-.308}{.2} \right) = P(z \le -1.54) = .5 - .4382$

$= .0618$

$\mu = 60.8$

$\beta = P(\bar{x} \le 60.392) = P\left(z \le \dfrac{60.392 - 60.8}{.2} \right) = P\left(z \le \dfrac{-.408}{.2} \right) = P(z \le -2.04) = .5 - .4793$

$= .0207$

$\mu = 60.9$

$$\beta = P(\bar{x} \le 60.392) = P\left(z \le \frac{60.392 - 60.9}{.2}\right) = P\left(z \le \frac{-.508}{.2}\right) = P(z \le -2.54) = .5 - .4945$$

$$= .0055$$

$$\mu = 61$$

$$\beta = P(\bar{x} \le 60.392) = P\left(z \le \frac{60.392 - 61}{.2}\right) = P\left(z \le \frac{-.608}{.2}\right) = P(z \le -3.04) = .5 - .4988$$

$$= .0012$$

    b.   No, $\beta = .2946$ when $\mu = 60.5$. Increase the sample size.

    c.   Plot is not included in this manual; power increase.

8.81 $H_0 : \mu \le 60$ versus $H_a : \mu \ge 60$, $\mu_0 = 60$

    $\alpha = .025$ and $\beta = .025$ for $\mu_a = 60.5$.

    $z^* = z_\alpha = z_{.025} = 1.96$

    $z_\beta = z_{.025} = 1.96$

$$n = \frac{(z^* + z_\beta)^2 \sigma^2}{(\mu_0 - \mu_a)^2} = \frac{(1.96 + 1.96)^2 (2)^2}{(60 - 60.5)^2} = \frac{(3.92)^2 (2)^2}{(-.5)^2} = 245.86248246 \text{ or } 246$$

8.83   Sampled population is normally distributed.

8.85   Explanations will vary.

8.87 $X^2 = \dfrac{(24)(.00014)}{.0005} = 6.72$

    $X^2_{.95} = 13.8484$

    Reject H_0

8.89 $\dfrac{(24)(.00014)}{45.5585}, \dfrac{(24)(.00014)}{9.88623} = [.0000738, .0003399]$

8.91   **a.** $H_0 : p \ge .05$ versus $H_a : p < .05$.

    b. $\hat{p} = \dfrac{18}{625} = .0288$

$$z = \frac{.0288 - .05}{\sqrt{\dfrac{(.05)(.95)}{625}}} = -2.43$$

        $-z_{.01} = -2.33, -z_{.001} = -3.09$

        Since $-3.09 < -2.43 \le -2.33$, reject H_0 at $\alpha = .10, .05, .01$, but not at $\alpha = .001$; very strong evidence.

    c. p-value $= P(z < -2.43) = .0075$

        Reject H_0 at $\alpha = .10, .05, .01$, but not at $\alpha = .001$.

    d.   Probably

8.93 **a.** p-value $= P(z < -2.63) = .0043$

b. Reject H_0 at $\alpha = .10, .05, .01$, but not at $\alpha = .001$.

c. Very strong evidence

8.95 **a.** $H_0 : \mu \leq 1200$ versus $H_a : \mu > 1200$

b. $t = \dfrac{1241.2 - 1200}{\dfrac{110.8}{\sqrt{35}}} = 2.20$

$t_{.05} = 1.691, t_{.01} = 2.441$

Since $1.691 < 2.20 < 2.441$, reject H_0 at $\alpha = .10, .05$, but not at $\alpha = .01$ or $.001$.

c. $t = \dfrac{1241.2 - 1200}{\dfrac{110.8}{\sqrt{100}}} = 3.72$

$t_{.001} = 3.175$

Since $3.72 > 3.175$, reject H_0 at each value of α. Sample of $n = 100$ provides stronger evidence.

d. Maybe, the two samples have equal point estimates of μ.

e. $t = \dfrac{1524.6 - 1200}{\dfrac{102.8}{\sqrt{35}}} = 18.68$

Reject H_0 at each value of α.
(1) Yes
(2) Most likely, $\bar{x}$ is much larger than 1200.

8.97 **a.** $\left[\hat{p} \pm z_{.025} \sqrt{\dfrac{\hat{p}(1 - \hat{p})}{n}} \right] = \left[.0288 \pm 1.96 \sqrt{\dfrac{(.0288)(.9712)}{625}} \right] = [.0157, .0419]$

b. $\left[\bar{x} \pm t_{.025} \dfrac{s}{\sqrt{n}} \right] = \left[23.663 \pm 2.032 \left(\dfrac{3.596}{\sqrt{50}} \right) \right] = [22.641, 24.685]$

c. $\left[1241.2 \pm 2.032 \left(\dfrac{110.8}{\sqrt{35}} \right) \right] = [1203.14, 1279.26]$

$\left[1241.2 \pm 1.984 \left(\dfrac{110.8}{\sqrt{100}} \right) \right] = [1219.217, 1263.183]$

$\left[1524.6 \pm 2.032 \left(\dfrac{102.8}{\sqrt{35}} \right) \right] = [1489.291, 1559.909]$

8.99 Fixed annuities:
a. $H_0 : \mu = 8.31\%$ versus $H_a : \mu \neq 8.31\%$.
b. $t = -6.66$
Reject H_0 at $\alpha = .05$.
Current mean return differs.

Domestic large cap stocks:
a. $H_0 : \mu = 11.71\%$ versus $H_a : \mu \neq 11.71\%$.
b. $t = .80$
Do not reject H_0 at $\alpha = .05$.
Current mean return does not differ.

Domestic MidCap Stocks:
a. $H_0 : \mu = 13.64\%$ versus $H_a : \mu \neq 13.64\%$.
b. $t = .53$
Do not reject H_0 at $\alpha = .05$.
Current mean return does not differ.

Domestic small cap stocks:
a. $H_0 : \mu = 14.93\%$ versus $H_a : \mu \neq 14.93\%$.
b. $t = 2.46$
Reject H_0 at $\alpha = .05$.
Current mean return differs.

8.101   Since $p = .078$ is $< .1$ there is some evidence.

Internet Exercise:

8.103   a. $H_0 : \mu = 1.19\%$, $H_a : \mu > 1.19\%$.
$$t = \frac{1.63 - 1.19}{.31 / \sqrt{12}} = 4.917$$

$t_{.05} = 1.796$ $t_{.025} = 2.201$ $t_{.005} = 3.106$ $t_{.0005} = 4.437$
So reject at all 4 values of α.

b.   Yes. Explanations will vary.

CHAPTER 9—Statistical Inferences Based on Two Samples

9.1   a. $\mu_1 < \mu_2$

　　b. $\mu_1 = \mu_2$

　　c. $\mu_1 < \mu_2$

　　d. $\mu_1 > \mu_2$

　　e. $\mu_1 > \mu_2$

　　f. $\mu_1 \neq \mu_2$

9.3   The samples do not influence each other.

9.5   a. $\bar{x}_1 = 25, \bar{x}_2 = 20, \sigma_1 = 3, \sigma_2 = 4, n_1 = 100, n_2 = 100$

$$\left[(25-20) \pm 1.96\sqrt{\frac{3^2}{100} + \frac{4^2}{100}} \right] = \left[5 \pm 1.96\sqrt{\frac{25}{100}} \right] = \left[5 \pm 1.96\left(\frac{5}{10}\right) \right] = [5 \pm .98] = [4.02, 5.98]$$

　　　Yes

　　b. $z = \dfrac{5-0}{.5} = 10$

　　　Reject H_0. Conclude $\mu_1 > \mu_2$.

　　c. $z = \dfrac{5-4}{.5} = 2$ and $z_{.05} = 1.645$

　　　p-value $= P(z > 2) = .0228$
　　　Reject H_0 at $\alpha = .10, .05$, but not at $\alpha = .01$ or .001.

9.7   a.

$$\left[(\bar{x}_1 - \bar{x}_2) \pm z_{\alpha/2}\sqrt{\frac{\sigma_1^2}{n_1} + \frac{\sigma_2^2}{n_2}} \right] = \left[(82.6 - 93) \pm 1.96\sqrt{\frac{(32.83)^2}{100} + \frac{(37.18)^2}{100}} \right]$$

$$= [-10.4 \pm 1.96(4.96)] = [-10.4 \pm 9.72] = [-20.12, -0.68]$$

　　　Yes; between .68 and 20.12 less

　　b. H_0: there is no difference in the mean audit delay for the two types of companies
　　　H_a: the mean audit delay for public owner-controlled companies is less than that for
　　　manager-controlled companies.

　　c. $z = \dfrac{-10.4 - 0}{4.96} = -2.0967$ and $-z_{.05} = -1.645$

　　　Reject H_0; conclude $\mu_1 < \mu_2$.

   d. p-value $= P(z < -2.1) = .0179$

       Reject H_0 at $\alpha = .10$ and $.05$, but not at $\alpha = .01$ or $.001$. There is strong evidence that $\mu_1 < \mu_2$.

9.9   **a.**
$$\left[(\bar{x}_1 - \bar{x}_2) \pm z_{\alpha/2} \sqrt{\frac{\sigma_1^2}{n_1} + \frac{\sigma_2^2}{n_2}} \right] = \left[(2.68 - 2.55) \pm 1.96 \sqrt{\frac{(.7)^2}{100} + \frac{(.6)^2}{100}} \right] = [.13 \pm 1.96(.092)]$$

$$= [.13 \pm .18] = [-.05, .31]$$

   b.   No

   c. $H_0 : \mu_1 - \mu_2 \le 0$ versus $H_a : \mu_1 - \mu_2 > 0$.

   d. $z = \dfrac{.13 - 0}{.092} = 1.41$ and $z_{.05} = 1.645$

       Do not reject H_0 at $\alpha = .05$. Cannot conclude $\mu_1 > \mu_2$.

9.11   **a.** $H_0 : \mu_1 - \mu_2 = 0$ versus $H_a : \mu_1 - \mu_2 \ne 0$.

   b. $z = \dfrac{8.2 - 7.3}{\sqrt{\dfrac{(1.6)^2}{125} + \dfrac{(1.4)^2}{175}}} = 5.06$

       $z_{.025} = 1.96$

       Since $5.06 > 1.96$, reject H_0 at $\alpha = .05$. Conclude μ_1 and μ_2 differ.

   c. p-value $= 2P(z > 5.06)$ is less than $.001$. Reject H_0 at each of the given values of α; extremely strong evidence.

   d.
$$\left[(8.2 - 7.3) \pm 2.575 \sqrt{\frac{(1.4)^2}{175} + \frac{(1.6)^2}{125}} \right] = [.9 \pm .458] = [.442, 1.358]$$

       μ_1 and μ_2 differ by between $.442$ and 1.358.

9.13   Sampled populations are approximately normal.

9.15   Sampled populations are normally distributed with equal variances.

9.17 $t = \dfrac{(\bar{x}_1 - \bar{x}_2) - D_0}{\sqrt{s_p^2 \left(\frac{1}{n_1} + \frac{1}{n_2} \right)}} = \dfrac{(240 - 210) - 20}{2.952} = \dfrac{10}{2.952} = 3.39$ and

       $t_{.01} = 2.681$ and $t_{.001} = 3.930$

       (with 12 df); reject H_0 at $\alpha = .10, .05, .01$, but not $\alpha = .001$; very strong evidence.

9.19 (9.16) $\bar{x}_1 = 240, \bar{x}_2 = 210, s_1 = 5, s_2 = 6, n_1 = n_2 = 7$

$$s_{\bar{x}_1-\bar{x}_2} = \sqrt{\frac{s_1^2}{n_1} + \frac{s_2^2}{n_2}} = \sqrt{\frac{25}{7} + \frac{36}{7}} = 2.952$$

$$df = \frac{\left(\dfrac{s_1^2}{n_1} + \dfrac{s_2^2}{n_2}\right)^2}{\dfrac{\left(\dfrac{s_1^2}{n_1}\right)^2}{n_1-1} + \dfrac{\left(\dfrac{s_2^2}{n_2}\right)^2}{n_2-1}} = \frac{\left(\dfrac{25}{7} + \dfrac{36}{7}\right)^2}{\dfrac{\left(\dfrac{25}{7}\right)^2}{6} + \dfrac{\left(\dfrac{36}{7}\right)^2}{6}} = \frac{75.939}{6.534}$$

= 11.6 so round down to 11 dfs.

95% CI = $(240 - 210) \pm t_{.025}(2.952) = 30 \pm (2.201)(2.952)$

= (23.503, 36.497)

(9.17) $t = \dfrac{(240 - 210) - 20}{2.952} = \dfrac{10}{2.952} = 3.39$

$t_{.01} = 2.718$ $t_{.001} = 4.025$ so reject H_0 for $\alpha = .1, .05,$ and $.01$. Fail to reject for $\alpha = .001$.

(9.18) $t = 3.39, df = 11$, so $t_{.005} = 3.106$ and $t_{.0005} = 4.437$

Reject at $\alpha = .1, .05,$ and $.01$. Fail to reject for $\alpha = .001$.

9.21 **a.** $H_0: \mu_A - \mu_B \leq 0$ versus $H_a: \mu_A - \mu_B > 0$

b. $s_p^2 = \dfrac{(11-1)(225)^2 + (11-1)(251)^2}{11+11-2} = 56813$

$t = \dfrac{(1500 - 1300) - 0}{\sqrt{56813\left(\dfrac{1}{11} + \dfrac{1}{11}\right)}} = \dfrac{200}{101.63} = 1.97$

$t_{.05} = 1.725$ and $t_{.01} = 2.528$ with 20 df

Since $1.725 < 1.97 < 2.528$, reject H_0 with $\alpha = .10$ and $.05$, but not with $\alpha = .01$ or $.001$

Strong evidence that $\mu_A - \mu_B > 0$.

c. $[(1500 - 1300) \pm 2.086(101.63)] = [200 \pm 212.01] = [-12.01, 412.01]$

9.23 **a.** $H_0 : \mu_O - \mu_I = 0$ versus $H_a : \mu_O - \mu_I \neq 0$

b. From the other there are 9 df.

$t_{.025} = 2.262$ and $t_{.005} = 3.25$

Since $2.262 < 2.31 < 3.25$, reject H_0 at $\alpha = .10, .05$, but not at $\alpha = .01, .001$.

There is strong evidence that H_0 is false.

c. $\left[(524 - 473) \pm t_{.025} \sqrt{\dfrac{(68)^2}{10} + \dfrac{(22)^2}{20}} \right]$

$= \left[51 \pm 2.262(22.059) \right] = [1.1, 100.9]$

9.25 The data for an independent samples experiment is collected using two independent samples, where the data for a paired difference test uses one sample that is tested twice.

9.27 Normally distributed population of paired differences

Large sample size (at least 30).

9.29 **a.** 95%: $\left[\bar{d} \pm t_{\alpha/2} \dfrac{s_d}{\sqrt{n}} \right] = \left[103.5 \pm 2.228 \left(\dfrac{5}{\sqrt{11}} \right) \right] = [103.5 \pm 3.359] = [100.141, 106.859]$; yes

99%: $\left[103.5 \pm 3.169 \left(\dfrac{5}{\sqrt{11}} \right) \right] = [103.5 \pm 4.777] = [98.723, 108.277]$; no

b. $t = \dfrac{103.5 - 100}{\dfrac{5}{\sqrt{11}}} = \dfrac{3.5}{1.50755} = 2.32$ and $t_{.05} = 1.812$ and $t_{.01} = 2.764$ with 10 df.

Reject H_0 at $\alpha = .05$ but not at $\alpha = .01$; strong evidence $\mu_1 - \mu_2 > 100$.

c. $t = \dfrac{103.5 - 110}{\dfrac{5}{\sqrt{11}}} = \dfrac{-6.5}{1.50755} = -4.31$ and $-t_{.05} = -1.812$ and $-t_{.01} = -2.764$ with 10 df.

Reject H_0 at $\alpha = .05$ and $.01$; very strong evidence $\mu_1 - \mu_2 < 110$.

9.31 **a.** $H_0 : \mu_d = 0$ versus $H_a : \mu_d \neq 0$.

b. $t = 9.22$ and $t_{.0005} = 5.041$

Reject H_0 at each value of α; extremely strong evidence.

c. p-value $= .00001 < \alpha = .001$

Reject H_0 at each value of α; extremely strong evidence.

d. $\left[\bar{d} \pm t_{\alpha/2} \dfrac{s_d}{\sqrt{n}} \right] = [.2237 \pm 2.306(.0242)] = [.1679, .2795]$

9.33 **a.** $d_1 = 3, d_2 = 5, d_3 = 2, d_4 = 4, d_5 = 1, d_6 = 4, d_7 = 5, d_8 = 2, \bar{d} = 3.25$

$$s_d^2 = \frac{\left(\begin{array}{c} (3-3.25)^2 + (5-3.25)^2 + (2-3.25)^2 + (4-3.25)^2 + (1-3.25)^2 + (4-3.25)^2 \\ + (5-3.25)^2 + (2-3.25)^2 \end{array} \right)}{7}$$

$$= 2.2143$$

$$s_d = 1.488$$

$$t = \frac{\bar{d}}{\dfrac{s_d}{\sqrt{n}}} = \frac{3.25}{\dfrac{1.488}{\sqrt{8}}} = 6.18$$

Since $t = 6.18 > t_{.025} = 2.365$, we reject $H_0 : \mu_d = 0$ in favor of $H_a : \mu_d \neq 0$ by setting $\alpha = .05$.

b. $\left[\bar{d} \pm t_{.025} \dfrac{s_d}{\sqrt{n}} \right] = \left[3.25 \pm 2.365 \left(\dfrac{1.488}{\sqrt{8}} \right) \right] = [3.25 \pm 1.2442] = [2.01, 4.49]$

Minimum: 2.01; maximum 4.49 (endpoints of 95% confidence interval for μ_d)

9.35 **a.** $H_0 : \mu_d = 0$, $H_a : \mu_d \neq 0$.

b. $t = 3.89$ and $t_{.005} = 3.499$ while $t_{.0005} = 5.408$ so we have very strong evidence.

c. p-value = .006 so again we have very strong evidence.

9.37 Sample sizes n_1 and n_2 are large; independent random samples.

9.39 $H_0 : p_1 - p_2 = 0$ versus $H_a : p_1 - p_2 \neq 0$.

$$\hat{p} = \frac{800 + 950}{2000} = .875$$

$$s_{\hat{p}_1 - \hat{p}_2} = \sqrt{.875(1-.875)\left(\frac{1}{1000} + \frac{1}{1000} \right)} = .01479$$

$$z = \frac{(.8 - .95) - 0}{.01479} = -10.14 \text{ and } -z_{.001} = -3.09$$

Reject H_0 at each value of α; extremely strong evidence.

9.41 **a.** $H_0 : p_1 - p_2 = 0$ versus $H_a : p_1 - p_2 \neq 0$.

b. $\hat{p} = \dfrac{142 + 122}{900} = .2933$

$$s_{\hat{p}_1 - \hat{p}_2} = \sqrt{.2933(1-.2933)\left(\frac{1}{400} + \frac{1}{500} \right)} = .03054$$

$$\hat{p}_1 = \frac{142}{400} = .355 \text{ and } \hat{p}_2 = \frac{122}{500} = .244$$

$$z = \frac{(.355 - .244) - 0}{.03054} = 3.63 \text{ and } z_{.0005} = 3.29$$

Reject H_0 at each value of α ; extremely strong evidence that the proportions differ.

c. $H_0 : p_1 - p_2 \le .05$ versus $H_a : p_1 - p_2 > .05$

$$s_{\hat{p}_1 - \hat{p}_2} = \sqrt{\frac{.355(1 - .355)}{400} + \frac{.244(1 - .244)}{500}} = .030681680$$

$$z = \frac{(.355 - .244) - .05}{.030681680} = 1.99$$

p-value $= P(z > 1.99) = .5 - .4767 = .0233$

Reject H_0 at $\alpha = .10$ and $\alpha = .05$; strong evidence

d. $[(.355 - .244) \pm 1.96(.030681680)] = [.111 \pm .0602] = [.0509, .1711]$
Yes, the entire interval is above zero.

9.43 $\hat{p}_1 = \frac{10}{500} = .02, \hat{p}_2 = \frac{27}{500} = .054$

$z = -2.85$ and p-value $= .004$

Reject H_0 at $\alpha = .10, .05, .01$, but not at $\alpha = .001$. Very strong evidence that p_1 and p_2 differ.

95% C.I. $[-0.0573036, -0.0106964]$; $-.0107$ smallest difference

9.45   a. $H_0 : p_1 - p_2 = 0$ versus $H_a : p_1 - p_2 \ne 0$

$$\hat{p}_1 = \frac{480}{500} = .96 \text{ and } \hat{p}_2 = \frac{450}{500} = .90$$

$$\hat{p} = \frac{480 + 450}{500 + 500} = .93$$

$$s_{\hat{p}_1 - \hat{p}_2} = \sqrt{.93(1 - .93)\left(\frac{1}{500} + \frac{1}{500}\right)} = .016136914$$

$$z = \frac{(.96 - .90) - 0}{.016136914} = 3.72 \text{ and } z_{.0005} = 3.291$$

Reject H_0 at $\alpha = .001$.

$$\left[(.96 - .90) \pm 1.96\sqrt{\frac{.96(1 - .96)}{500} + \frac{.90(1 - .90)}{500}}\right] = [.06 \pm 1.96(.01602)]$$

$$= [.06 \pm .031] = [.029, .091]$$

Largest: .091, smallest: .029

b. $H_0 : p_1 - p_2 = 0$ versus $H_a : p_1 - p_2 \neq 0$

$$\hat{p}_1 = \frac{200}{500} = .40, \hat{p}_2 = \frac{270}{500} = .54$$

$$\hat{p} = \frac{200 + 270}{500 + 500} = .47$$

$$s_{\hat{p}_1 - \hat{p}_2} = \sqrt{.47(1 - .47)\left(\frac{1}{500} + \frac{1}{500}\right)} = .031565804$$

$$z = \frac{(.40 - .54) - 0}{.031565804} = -4.435 \text{ and } -z_{.0005} = -3.291$$

Reject H_0 at $\alpha = .001$.

$$\left[(.40 - .54) \pm 1.96\sqrt{\frac{.40(1 - .40)}{500} + \frac{.54(1 - .54)}{500}} \right] = [-.14 \pm 1.96(.0312538)]$$

$$= [-.14 \pm .061] = [-.201, -.079]$$

Largest: –.079, smallest: –.201

9.47 Explanations will vary (s_1^2 will be larger than s_2^2 which estimates α_1^2 is larger than α_2^2).

9.49 a. 2.96

b. 4.68

c. 3.16

d. 8.81

9.51 a. $F = \frac{s_2^2}{s_1^2} = \frac{9^2}{5^2} = \frac{81}{25} = 3.24$

$F_{.025} = 8.66$ with $df_1 = 16 - 1 = 15$ and $df_2 = 5 - 1 = 4$

Do not reject $H_0 : \sigma_1^2 = \sigma_2^2$, since $F = 3.24 < F_{.025} = 8.66$

b. $F = \frac{s_2^2}{s_1^2} = \frac{9^2}{5^2} = 3.24$

$F_{.01} = 14.20$ with $df_1 = 16 - 1 = 15$ and $df_2 = 5 - 1 = 4$

Do not reject $H_0 : \sigma_1^2 \geq \sigma_2^2$, since $F = 3.24 < F_{.01} = 14.20$

9.53 a. $F = 2.06$ with $df_1 = 7$ and $df_2 = 4$.

$F_{.025} = 9.07$

Since $2.06 < 9.07$ do not reject H_0 at alpha = 0.05

b. *p*-value = 0.5052 > alpha = 0.05 so do not reject H_0 at alpha = 0.05

c. Yes

d. $F = s_2^2 / s_1^2 = 0.337598 / 0.16373 = 2.06$

9.55 **a.** $H_0 : \mu_T - \mu_B = 0$ versus $H_a : \mu_T - \mu_B \neq 0$.

$$t = \frac{\bar{x}_1 - \bar{x}_2}{\sqrt{\frac{s_1^2}{n_1} + \frac{s_2^2}{n_2}}}$$

$$t = \frac{1.52 - 1.20}{\sqrt{\frac{.92^2}{36} + \frac{.84^2}{36}}} = \frac{.32}{\sqrt{.043111}} = 1.54$$

α	2-sided rejection point
.10	± 1.669
.05	± 1.995
.01	± 2.648
.001	± 3.437

Cannot reject H_0 at any of the given values of α; little or no evidence.

b.
$$\left[(\bar{x}_1 - \bar{x}_2) \pm t_{\alpha/2} \sqrt{\frac{s_1^2}{n_1} + \frac{s_2^2}{n_2}} \right] = [(1.52 - 1.20) \pm 1.995(.2076)]$$

$$= [.32 \pm .41] = [-.09, .73]$$

9.57 **a.** $H_0 : \mu_d = \mu_B - \mu_A \leq 0$ versus $H_a : \mu_d = \mu_B - \mu_A > 0$.

b. $t = 10.00$ so we reject all values of α. $t_{.10} = 1.363$, $t_{.05} = 1.796$, $t_{.01} = 2.718$, $t_{.001} = 4.025$.

Extremely strong evidence.

c. p-value ≈ 0 so reject at all values of α.

Extremely strong evidence.

9.59 $\bar{x}_1 = 189, s_1 = 12, \bar{x}_2 = 145, s_2 = 10$

$$s_p^2 = \frac{(6-1)(12)^2 + (12-1)(10)^2}{6+12-2} = \frac{1820}{16} = 113.75$$

a. $H_0 : \mu_O - \mu_{JVC} = 0$ versus $H_a : \mu_O - \mu_{JVC} \neq 0$.

$$t = \frac{(189-145) - 0}{\sqrt{113.75\left(\frac{1}{6} + \frac{1}{12}\right)}} = 8.251 \text{ and } t_{.0005} = 4.015 \text{ with 16 df}$$

Reject H_0 with $\alpha = .001$; extremely strong evidence

b.
$$\left[(189-145) \pm t_{.025} \sqrt{113.75\left(\frac{1}{6} + \frac{1}{12}\right)} \right] = [44 \pm 2.120(5.33)] = [44 \pm 11.31]$$

$$= [32.69, 55.31]; \text{ probably}$$

c. $H_0 : \mu_0 - \mu_{JVC} \leq 30$ versus $H_a : \mu_0 - \mu_{JVC} > 30$

$t = \dfrac{44 - 30}{5.33} = 2.627$; reject H_0 at $\alpha = .05$ since $t_{.05} = 1.746$ with 16 df.

Internet Exercises

9.61   a. $H_0 : p_W = p_M$ versus $H_a : p_W \neq p_M$

$\hat{p} = .63$

$$s_{p_W - p_M} = \sqrt{.63(1 - .63)\left(\dfrac{1}{520} + \dfrac{1}{563}\right)} = .02936$$

$$z = \dfrac{.66 - .59}{.02936} = \dfrac{.07}{.02936} = 2.384$$

p-value $= 2(.5 - .4914) = .0172$

Reject H_0, there is sufficient reason to believe that opinions on campaign finance reform differs between males and females.

Results significant at $\alpha = .05$ but not at .01.

b.   Selection of political poll will vary with date of access to any of the web sites listed. Explanations of results will vary.

CHAPTER 10—Experimental Design and Analysis of Variance

10.1 factor = Independent variables in a designed experiment

treatments = Values of a factor (or combination of factors)

experimented units = The entities to which the treatments are assigned

response variable = The variable of interest in an experiment; dependent variable

10.3 Response: time to stabilize emergency condition
Factor: display panels
Treatments: panels A, B, C
Experimental units: controllers.

10.5 Constant variance, normality, independence

10.7 If the one-way ANOVA F test leads us to conclude that at least two of the treatment means differ, then we wish to investigate which of the treatment means differ and we wish to estimate how large the differences are.

10.9 **a.** F = 184.57, p-value = .000: Reject H_0. Shelf location has different effects on sales.

b. $(\bar{X}_B - \bar{x}_M) \pm q_{.05}\sqrt{\dfrac{MSE}{m}} = (55.8 - 77.2) \pm 3.67\sqrt{\dfrac{6.16}{6}} = -21.4 \pm 3.72$

bottom-middle: −21.4, [−25.12,−17.68]
bottom-top: 4.3, [.58, 8.02]
middle-top: 25.7, [21.98, 29.42]
Middle shelf maximizes the differences

c. $(\bar{X}_B - \bar{x}_M) \pm t_{.025}\sqrt{MSE\left(\dfrac{1}{6} + \dfrac{1}{6}\right)} = (55.8 - 77.2) \pm 2.131\sqrt{6.16\left(\dfrac{1}{3}\right)} = -21.4 \pm 3.05$

bottom-middle: [−24.45,−18.35]
bottom-top: [1.25, 7.35]
middle-top: [22.65, 28.75]

d. $(\bar{X}_B) \pm t_{.025}\sqrt{MSE\left(\dfrac{1}{6}\right)} = (55.8) \pm 2.131\sqrt{6.16\left(\dfrac{1}{6}\right)} = 55.8 \pm 2.16$

bottom: [53.65, 57.96]
middle: [75.04, 79.36]
top: [49.34, 53.66]

10.11 **a.** F = 43.36, p-value = .000; Reject H_0: bottle design does have an impact on sales.

b. $\mu_B - \mu_A : \left[16.2 \pm (3.77)\sqrt{\dfrac{7.5667}{5}}\right] = [11.56, 20.84]$

$\mu_C - \mu_A : [3.56, 12.84]$
$\mu_C - \mu_B : [-12.64, -3.36]$

c. (1) $[16.2 \pm (2.179)(1.73973178)] = [12.41, 19.99]$
(2) $[4.41, 11.99]$
(3) $[-11.79, -4.21]$

d. $\mu_A : 16.60, [13.92, 19.28]$
$\mu_B : 32.8, [30.12, 35.48]$
$\mu_C : 24.8, [22.12, 27.48]$

10.13 Tukey $q_{.05} = 4.05$, MSE = 606.15, m = 5
Divot – Alpha: $(336.6 - 253.6) \pm 44.59$: $[38.41, 127.59]$
Divot – Century: $(336.6 - 241.8) \pm 44.59$: $[50.21, 139.39]$
Divot – Best: $(336.6 - 306.4) \pm 44.59$: $[-14.39, 74.79]$
Century – Alpha: $(241.8 - 253.6) \pm 44.59$: $[-56.39, 32.79]$
Century – Best: $(241.8 - 306.4) \pm 44.59$: $[-109.19, -20.01]$
Best – Alpha: $(306.4 - 253.6) \pm 44.59$: $[8.21, 97.39]$
Best and Divot appear to be the most durable

$t_{.025} = 2.120$, MSE = 606.16, n = 5
Divot: 336.6 ± 23.34 $[313.26, 359.94]$
Best: 306.4 ± 23.34 $[283.06, 329.74]$
Alpha: $253.6 \pm 23.34 = [230.26, 276.94]$
Century: $241.8 \pm 23.34 [218.46, 265.14]$

10.15 Use when there are differences between the experimental units that are concealing any true differences between the treatments.

10.17 a. $F = 36.23$, p-value = .000; Reject H_0: there is a difference in sales methods

b. $F = 12.87$, p-value = .007; Reject H_0: salesmen do have an effect on sales

c. $(\bar{X}_1 - \bar{X}_2) \pm q_{.05} \dfrac{s}{\sqrt{b}} = (\bar{X}_1 - \bar{X}_2) \pm 4.90 \left(\dfrac{.928}{\sqrt{3}}\right) = (\bar{X}_1 - \bar{X}_2) \pm 2.63$

Method 1 – Method 2: $(30.33 - 30) \pm 2.63 = [-2.30, 2.96]$
Method 1 – Method 3: $(30.33 - 25.33) \pm 2.63 = [2.37, 7.63]$
Method 1 –Method 4: $(30.33 - 24) \pm 2.63 = [3.70, 8.96]$
Method 2 – Method 3: $(30 - 25.33) \pm 2.63 = [2.04, 7.30]$
Method 2 – Method 4: $(30 - 24) \pm 2.63 = [3.37, 8.63]$
Method 3 – Method 4: $(25.33 - 24) \pm 2.63 = [-1.30, 3.96]$
Appears that Method I and 2 maximize mean weekly sales.

10.19 a,b MINITAB output:
Analysis of Variance for Keyboard experiment

Source	DF	SS	MS	F	P
Brand	2	392.667	196.333	441.75	0.000
Speciali	3	143.583	47.861	107.69	0.000
Error	6	2.667	0.444		
Total	11	538.917			

both keyboard brand and the specialist have a significant impact on the mean number of words entered.

    c.   Tukey $q_{.05} = 4.34$, MSE $= .444$, s $= .666$, b $= 4$

        AB: $(72.25 - 62.25) \pm 4.34\ (.666\ /\ 2) = 10 \pm 1.45 = [8.55,\ 11.45]$

        AC: $(72.25 - 58.75) \pm 1.45\ [12.05,\ 14.95]$

        BC: $(62.25 - 58.75) \pm 1.45\ [2.05,\ 4.95]$

        Keyboard A maximizes the mean number of words entered per minute.

10.21 **a.**   F $= 5.78$, *p*-value $= .0115$; Reject H_0: the soft drinks differ in terms of mean sales.

    b.   Tukey $q_{.05} = 3.61$, MSE $= 691$, s $= 26.287$, b $= 10$

        Coke Classic – New Coke: $(102.8 - 64.8) \pm 3.61\ (26.287\ /\ 3.162) = 38 \pm 30.01$
        $= [7.99,\ 68.01]$

        Coke Classic – Pepsi: $(102.8 - 73.5) \pm 30.01 = [-.71,\ 59.31]$

        New Coke – Pepsi: $(64.8 - 73.5) \pm 30.01 = [-38.71,\ 21.31]$

    c.   Yes; mean sales for New Coke are less than Pepsi, even though the Tukey test indicates this difference is not significant.

10.23 **a.**   F $=$ MST / MSE $= 35.755\ /\ 7.65 = 4.67$. $F_{.05} = 3.22$ approximately with $df_1 = 2$, $df_2 = 42$: Reject H_0

    b.   Tukey $q_{.05} = 3.43$ (approximated from table A.9), MSE $= 7.65$, m $= 15$

        Group 1 – Group 2: $(6.7 - 9.7) \pm 2.45$: $[-5.45,\ -.55]$

        Group 1 – control: $(6.7 - 7.6) \pm 2.45$: $[-3.35,\ 1.55]$

        Group 2 – control: $(9.7 - 6.7) \pm 2.45$: $[.55,\ 5.45]$

        Group 2 is the largest.

10.25   Computer model effects differ (*p*-value $= .0002$) and compiler effects differ (*p*-value $= .0001$) $t_{.025} = 2.776$ with 4 degrees of freedom.

    $\mu_{3h} - \mu_{1h}$: $[-3.07 \pm 2.776(.144)] = [-3.07 \pm .3997] = [-3.47,\ -2.67]$

    $\mu_{2h} - \mu_{1h}$: $[-1.87 \pm .3997] = [-2.27,\ -1.47]$

    $\mu_{3h} - \mu_{2h}$: $[-1.20 \pm .3997] = [-1.60,\ -.80]$

    $\mu_{l435} - \mu_{l235}$: $[.87 \pm 2.776(.144)] = [.87 \pm .3997] = [.47,\ 1.27]$

    $\mu_{l335} - \mu_{l235}$: $[2.40 \pm .3997] = [2.00,\ 2.80]$

    $\mu_{l435} - \mu_{l335}$: $[-1.53 \pm .3997] = [-1.93,\ -1.13]$

CHAPTER 11—Chi-Square Tests

11.1 (1) We perform an experiment in which we carry out n identical trials and in which there are k possible outcomes on each trial.

    (2) The probabilities of the k outcomes are denoted, p_1, p_2, ..., p_k where $p_1 + p_2 + \cdots + p_k = 1$. These probabilities stay the same from trial to trial.

    (3) The trials in the experiment are independent.

    (4) The results of the experiment are observed counts of the number of trials that result in each of the k possible outcomes. The counts are denoted n_1, n_2, ..., n_k. That is, n_1 is the number of trials resulting in the first possible outcome, n_2 is the number of trials resulting in the second possible outcome, and so forth.

11.3 Explanations will vary.

11.5 Using classes of a histogram or using intervals from the empirical rule.

11.7   **a.** each expected value is ≥ 5

    b.

$$X^2 = \Sigma\left(\frac{(182-300)^2}{300} + \frac{(536-380)^2}{380} + \frac{(354-440)^2}{440} + \frac{(151-320)^2}{320} + \frac{(777-560)^2}{560}\right) = 300.605$$

$$X^2_{.10} = 7.779$$

    since $300.605 > 7.779$, reject H_0. The viewing shares of the current rating period differ from those of the last.

11.9   **a.**

$$X^2 = \Sigma\left(\frac{(131-200)^2}{200} + \frac{(273-200)^2}{200} + \frac{(119-200)^2}{200} + \frac{(301-200)^2}{200} + \frac{(176-200)^2}{200} + \frac{(200-200)^2}{200}\right) = 137.14$$

$$X^2_{.025} = 12.8325$$

    Reject H_0.

    b.   differences between brand preferences

11.11   **a.** $\bar{x} = 18.1077$, $s = 3.9612$

    $\bar{x} - 2s = 18.1077 - 2(3.9612) = 10.185$

    $\bar{x} - s = 18.1077 - 3.9612 = 14.147$

    $\bar{x} + s = 18.1077 + 3.9612 = 22.069$

    $\bar{x} + 2s = 18.1077 + 2(3.9612) = 26.030$

    (1) $[-\infty, 10.185]$

    (2) $[10.185, 14.147]$

    (3) $[14.147, 18.108]$

    (4) $[18.108, 22.069]$

    (5) $[22.069, 26.030]$

    (6) $[26.030, \infty]$

b. (1) For instance, $P(x < 10.185) = P\left(z < \dfrac{10.185 - 18.1077}{3.9612}\right) = P(z < -2) = .5 - .4772 = .0228$

    and $E_1 = .0228(65) = 1.482. \approx 1.5$

(2) $.1359$, $E_2 = 8.8335 \approx 9$

(3) $.3413$, $E_3 = 22.1845 \approx 22$

(4) $.3413$, $E_4 = 22.1845 \approx 22$

(5) $.1359$, $E_5 = 8.8335 \approx 9$

(6) $.0228$, $E_6 = 1.482 \approx 1.5$

c. We can use the chi-square test since the average of the E_i values is 10.833 (which is ≥ 5) and since the smallest E_i value is 1.482 (which is ≥ 1).

d. H_0: the probabilities that a randomly selected payment time will be in intervals 1, 2, 3, 4, 5, and 6 are $p_1 = .0228$, $p_2 = .1359$, $p_3 = .3413$, $p_4 = .3413$, $p_5 = .1359$, and $p_6 = .0228$ versus
H_a: the above null hypothesis is not true.

e. 1, 9, 30, 15, 8, 2

$$\chi^2 = \frac{(1-1.5)^2}{1.5} + \frac{(9-9)^2}{9} + \frac{(30-22)^2}{22} + \frac{(15-22)^2}{22} + \frac{(8-9)^2}{9} + \frac{(2-1.5)^2}{1.5}$$

$$= .167 + 0 + 2.909 + 2.227 + .111 + .167$$
$$= 5.581$$

f. Fail to reject H_0 since $5.581 < \chi^2_{.05} = 7.81473$ (with $6 - 1 - 2 = 3$ degrees of freedom). Conclude normality.

11.13

Interval		n_i	E_i	$\dfrac{(n_i - E_i)^2}{E_i}$
$< \bar{x} - 2s$	$[-\infty, .51]$	1	$.0228(100) = 2.28$	.719
$\bar{x} - 2s < \bar{x} - s$	$[.51, 2.985]$	16	$.1359(100) = 13.59$	.427
$\bar{x} - s < \bar{x}$	$[2.985, 5.46]$	36	$.3413(100) = 34.13$	.102
$\bar{x} < \bar{x} + s$	$[5.46, 7.935]$	30	$.3413(100) = 34.13$	.500
$\bar{x} + s < \bar{x} + 2s$	$[7.935, 10.41]$	14	$.1359(100) = 13.59$	.012
$> \bar{x} + 2s$	$[10.41, \infty]$	3	$.0228(100) = 2.28$	.227

$\chi^2 = .719 + .427 + .102 + .5 + .012 + .227 = 1.987$

Since $1.987 < \chi^2_{.10} = 6.25139$ (with $6 - 1 - 2 = 3$ degrees of freedom), we do not reject H_0: normality. Conclude waiting times normal.

11.15 Studying the relationship between two variables

11.17 **a.**

8	32	40
12	48	60
20	80	100

b.

16% 40% 80%	24% 60% 30%
4% 6.67% 20%	56% 93.33% 70%

c.

$$\chi^2 = \frac{(16-8)^2}{8} + \frac{(24-32)^2}{32} + \frac{(4-12)^2}{12} + \frac{(56-48)^2}{48}$$
$$= 8 + 2 + 5.333 + 1.333 = 16.667$$

H_0: whether a person drinks wine and whether a person watches tennis are independent versus H_a: dependent. Since $16.667 > \chi^2_{.05} = 3.84146$ (with $(2-1)(2-1) = 1$ degree of freedom), we reject H_0. Conclude dependent.

d. Explanations will vary. Probably.

11.19 **a.** row total

24.24%

22.73%

53.03%

col total   51.515%   48.485%

b.

18.18% 75% 35.29%	6.06% 25% 12.5%
13.64% 60% 26.47%	9.09% 40% 18.75%
19.7% 37.14% 38.24%	33.3% 62.86% 68.75%

c. $\chi^2 = 6.86$, *p*-value=.032, Cannot reject H_0 at .01 level

d. There is no difference between smokers and nonsmokers at the .01 level, but can reject H_0 at α=.05 so a difference is possible.

11.21 a.
$$X^2 = \frac{(37-53.5)^2}{53.5} + \frac{(48-53.5)^2}{53.5} + \frac{(56-53.5)^2}{53.5} + \frac{(73-53.5)^2}{53.5}$$
$$+ \frac{(213-196.5)^2}{196.5} + \frac{(202-196.5)^2}{196.5} + \frac{(194-196.5)^2}{196.5} + \frac{(177-196.5)^2}{196.5} = 16.385$$
$$X_{.05}^2 = 7.815 \text{ with 3 degrees of freedom}$$

Since $16.385 > 7.815$, reject H_0: independence

b. $(.148 - .292) \pm 1.96\sqrt{\dfrac{.148(.852)}{250} + \dfrac{.292(.708)}{250}} = -.144 \pm .0715 = [-.216, -.072]$

11.23 $\chi^2 = \dfrac{(30-60)^2}{60} + \dfrac{(91-60)^2}{60} + \dfrac{(97-60)^2}{60} + \dfrac{(40-60)^2}{60} + \dfrac{(42-60)^2}{60}$

$= 15 + 16.02 + 22.82 + 6.67 + 5.4$

$= 65.91$

Since $65.91 > \chi_{.05}^2 = 9.48773$ (with $5-1=4$ degrees of freedom), we reject H_0: $p_1 = p_2 = p_3 = p_4 = p_5 = .2$; entrances not equally used.

95% C.I.: $\left[.323 \pm 1.96\sqrt{\dfrac{.323(.677)}{299}} \right] = [.27, .376]$

11.25 a.

Buyers	Style		
	European	Japanese	Total
First-time	8	32	40
Repeat	40	20	60
Total	48	52	100

b. $X^2 = \dfrac{(8-19.2)^2}{19.2} + \dfrac{(32-20.8)^2}{20.8} + \dfrac{(40-28.8)^2}{28.8} + \dfrac{(20-31.2)^2}{31.2} = 20.940$

$X_{.05}^2 = 3.841$ with 1 degrees of freedom

Since $20.940 > 3.841$, reject H_0: independence.

c. Graph not included in this manual. Dependent, explanations will vary.

11.27 Chi-square = 71.476, *p*-value = .000

Reject H_0: independence

Internet Exercise:

11.29 H_0: There is no difference by Ethnic Group

Ha: There is a difference by Ethnic Group

Chi-square Contingency Table Test for Independence

		Yes	No	Total
White	Observed	**1285**	**2070**	3355
	% of row	38.3%	61.7%	100.0%
	% of column	84.8%	78.4%	80.7%
	% of total	30.9%	49.8%	80.7%
Black	Observed	**131**	**344**	475
	% of row	27.6%	72.4%	100.0%
	% of column	8.6%	13.0%	11.4%
	% of total	3.2%	8.3%	11.4%
Hispanic	Observed	**100**	**227**	327
	% of row	30.6%	69.4%	100.0%
	% of column	6.6%	8.6%	7.9%
	% of total	2.4%	5.5%	7.9%
Total	Observed	1516	2641	4157
	% of row	36.5%	63.5%	100.0%
	% of column	100.0%	100.0%	100.0%
	% of total	36.5%	63.5%	100.0%

25.96 chi-square
2 df
2.31E-06 p-value

Reject H_0. There is a difference by Ethnic Group at the .01 level of significance.

CHAPTER 12—Simple Linear Regression Analysis

12.1   When there appears to be a linear relationship between y and x

12.3 β_1: the change in the mean value of the dependent variable that is associated with a one-unit increase in the value of the independent variable
β_0: the mean value of the dependent variable when the value of the independent variable is zero

12.5   The straight line appearance of this data plot suggests that the simple linear regression model with a positive slope might be appropriate.

12.7   The straight line appearance on this data plot suggest that the simple linear regression model with a positive slope might be appropriate.

12.9   The plot looks reasonably linear.

12.11   **a.**

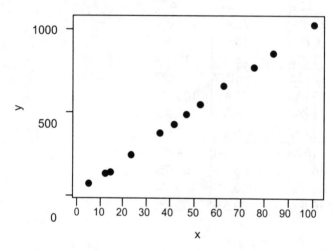

   b.   Yes, the plot looks linear, positive slope

12.13   **a.**

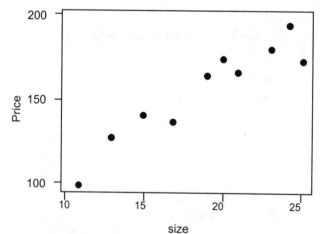

   b.   Yes, the relationship looks to be linear with a positive slope.

12.15   The quality or "goodness" of the fit of the least squares line to the observed data.

12.17 Evaluate $\hat{y} = b_0 + b_1 x$ for the given value of x.

12.19 a. $b_0 = 14.82$ $b_1 = 5.707$

The interpretation of b_0 is the starting salary of someone with a GPA of 0.

The interpretation of b_1 is for each increase in GPA of 1, salary goes up $5,707

No. The interpretation of b_0 does not make practical sense since it indicates that someone with a GPA = 0 would have a starting salary of $14,816, when in fact they would not have graduated with a GPA = 0.

b. $\hat{y} = 14.82 + 5.707(3.25) = 33.36775$

That is, $33,367.75

12.21 a. $b_0 = 7.814$ $b_1 = 2.665$

b_0 – 0 price difference yields demand of 7.814.

b_1 – each increase in 1 of price difference increases demand on average by 2.665.

Yes. The interpretation of b_0 does make practical sense since it indicates that 781,409 bottles of detergent would be demanded when the price difference with other products is zero.

b. $\hat{y} = 7.814 + 2.665\,(.10) = 8.0805$

c.

$\hat{y} = b_0 + b_1 x$

$8.5 = 7.81409 + 2.6652x$

$x = \dfrac{.68591}{2.6652} = .257, \text{or about 26 cents}$

12.23 a. MINITAB output

Regression Analysis: Sale Price versus Size

```
The regression equation is
Sale Price = 48.0 + 5.70 Size

Predictor     Coef       SE Coef        T          P
Constant      48.02      14.41          3.33       0.010
Size          5.7003     0.7457         7.64       0.000

S = 10.59       R-Sq = 88.0%       R-Sq(adj) = 86.5%
```

b. b_1 is the estimated increase in mean sales price (5.700) for every hundred square foot increase in home size.

b_0 is the estimated mean sales price when square footage = 0. No, the interpretation of b_0 makes no practical sense.

c. $\hat{y} = 48.02 + 5.700x$.

d. $\hat{y} = 48.02 + 5.700\,(20) = 162.02$.

That is, $162,020.

12.25 σ^2; σ That is, the constant variance and standard deviation of the error term populations.

12.27 $s^2 = \dfrac{SSE}{n-2} = \dfrac{191.7017}{11-2} = 21.3002$

$s = \sqrt{s^2} = \sqrt{21.30018} = 4.61521$

12.29 $s^2 = \dfrac{746.7624}{10} = 74.67624, s = 8.64154$

12.31 $s^2 = \dfrac{SSE}{n-2} = \dfrac{222.8242}{10-2} = 27.8530$

$s = \sqrt{s^2} = \sqrt{27.8530} = 5.2776$

12.33 Explanations will vary.

12.35 a. $b_0 = 11.4641$ $b_1 = 24.6022$

b. $SSE = 191.7017$ $s^2 = 21.3002$ $s = 4.615$

c. $s_{b_1} = .8045$ $t = 30.580$

$t = b_1 / s_{b_1} = 24.602 / .8045 = 30.580$

d. $df = 9$ $t_{.025} = 2.262$ Reject H_0, strong evidence of a significant relationship between x and y.

e. $t_{.005} = 3.250$ Reject H_0, very strong evidence of a significant relationship between x and y.

f. p-value $= .000$ Reject at all α, extremely strong evidence of a significant relationship between x and y.

g. $[24.6022 \pm 2.262(.8045)] = [22.782, 26.422]$

h. $[24.6022 \pm 3.250(.8045)] = [21.987, 27.217]$

i. $s_{b_0} = 3.4390$ $t = 3.334$

$t = b_0 / s_{b_0} = 11.464 / 3.439 = 3.334$

j. p-value $= .0087$ Reject at all α except .001

k. $s_{b_1} = \dfrac{s}{\sqrt{SS_{xx}}} = \dfrac{4.61521}{\sqrt{32.909}} = .8045$

$$s_{b_0} = s\sqrt{\dfrac{1}{n} + \dfrac{\overline{x}^2}{SS_{xx}}} = 4.61521\sqrt{\dfrac{1}{11} + \dfrac{3.909^2}{32.909}} = 3.439$$

12.37 See the solutions to 11.34 for guidance.

a. $b_0 = 18.488$, $b_1 = 10.1463$

b. SSE $= 746.7624$, $s^2 = 74.67624$, $s = 8.642$

c. $s_{b_1} = .0866$, $t = 117.1344$

d. Reject H_0.

e. Reject H_0.

f. p-value $= .000$; reject H_0 at each value of α

g. $[10.1463 \pm 2.228(.0866)] = [9.953, 10.339]$

h. $[10.1463 \pm 3.169(.0866)] = [9.872, 10.421]$

i. $s_{b_0} = 4.677$, $t = 3.95$

j. p-value $= .003$; fail to reject H_0 at $\alpha = .001$. Reject H_0 at all other values of α

k. $s_{b_1} = \dfrac{s}{\sqrt{SS_{xx}}} = \dfrac{8.64154}{\sqrt{9952.667}} = .086621$

$$s_{b_0} = s\sqrt{\dfrac{1}{n} + \dfrac{\overline{x}^2}{SS_{xx}}} = 8.64154\sqrt{\dfrac{1}{12} + \dfrac{45.667^2}{9952.667}} = 4.67658$$

12.39 Find s_{b1} from Minitab

```
        The regression equation is
      sales = 66.2 + 4.43 ad exp

      Predictor        Coef       SE Coef           T          P
      Constant       66.212         5.767       11.48      0.000
      Ad exp         4.4303        0.5810        7.62      0.000
```

95% C.I. for β_1 $[\,4.4303 \pm 2.306(.5810)\,] = [3.091, 5.770]$

12.41 The distance between x_0 and $\overline{x}$, the average of the previously observed values of x.

12.43 The smaller the distance value, the shorter the lengths of the intervals.

12.45 **a.** 109.873, [106.721, 113.025]

b. 109.873, [98.967, 120.779]

c. We have x = 4, $\bar{x} = 3.90$, $SS_{xx} = 32.90$, $n = 11$

distance value $= \dfrac{1}{11} + \dfrac{(4-3.90)^2}{32.90} = 0.090657961$

So confidence interval is:

$109.873 \pm (2.262)(4.615)\sqrt{0.090657961} = \left[106.729, 113.016\right]$

this compares (within rounding) to the computer generated output.

For the prediction interval with the same quantities we get

$109.873 \pm (2.262)(4.615)\sqrt{1.090657961}$

$= [98.971, 120.775]$ which also compares within rounding.

d. 113 minutes

12.47 **a.** 627.26, [621.05, 633.47]

b. 627.26, [607.03, 647.49]

c. $s\sqrt{dist} = 2.7868, s = 8.642, dist = \left(\dfrac{2.79}{8.642}\right)^2 = .104000$

99% C.I.: $[627.26 \pm 3.169(2.79)] = [(618.42, 636.10)]$

99% P.I.: $[627.26 \pm 3.169(8.642)\sqrt{1.104227}] = [598.48, 656.04]$

12.49 2.3429, [1.7369, 2.9489]

12.51 From Megastat

Regression output — confidence interval

Variables	coefficients	std. Error	t(df = 8)	p-value	95% lower	95% upper
Intercept	66.2121	5.7667	11.482	3.00E-06	52.9141	79.5102
Advertising	4.4303	0.5810	7.625	.0001	3.0904	5.7702

Predicted values for: Sales — confidence interval

		95% Confidence Intervals		95% Prediction Intervals		
Advertising	Predicted	lower	upper	lower	upper	Leverage
11	114.945	110.604	119.287	102.024	127.867	0.127
15	132.667	124.353	140.980	117.928	147.405	0.467

The regression equation is:

Sales = 66.2121 + 4.4303 (Advertising)

a. $\hat{y} = b_0 + b_1(11) = 66.2121 + 4.4303(11) = 114.945$
95% C.I.: [110.604, 119.287]

b. 114.945
95% P.I.: [102.024, 127.867]

12.53 Proportion of the total variation in the n observed values of y that is explained by the simple linear regression model.

12.55 Explained variation = 20,110.5445 – 191.7017 = 19918.8428

$r^2 = 19918.8428 / 20110.5445 = 0.990$

$r = +\text{sqrt}(0.990) = 0.995$

99% of the variation in service time can be explained by variation in number of copiers repaired.

12.57 Explained variation = 1,025,339.6667 – 746.7624 = 1,024,592.904

$r^2 = 1024592.904 / 1025339.6667 == 0.999$

$r = +\text{sqrt}(0.999) = 0.9995$

99.9% of the variation in direct labor can be explained by variation in batch size.

12.59 Explained variation = 5.1817

Unexplained variation = 0.1343

Total variation = 5.3160

$r^2 = .975$

97.5% of the variation in overall rating can be explained by variation in taste rating.

12.61 Calculate $t = \dfrac{r\sqrt{n-2}}{\sqrt{1-r^2}}$ and obtain its associated p-value. If p-value $< \alpha$ then you reject.

12.63 Reject H_0 at all four values of α.

12.65 t–test on β_1

12.67 **a.** F = 19918.844 / (191.7017 / 9) = 935.149

b. $F_{.05} = 5.12$ $df_1 = 1$, $df_2 = 9$

Since 935.149 > 5.12, reject H_0 with strong evidence of a significant relationship between x and y.

c. $F_{.01} = 10.56$ $df_1 = 1$, $df_2 = 9$

Since 935.149 > 10.56, reject H_0 with very strong evidence of a significant relationship between x and y.

   d.   *p*-value =less than .001; Reject H_0 at all levels of α, extremely strong evidence of a significant relationship between x and y.

   e. $t^2 = (30.58)^2 = 935.14$ (approximately equals F = 935.149)

   $(t_{.025})^2 = (2.262)^2 = 5.12 = F_{.05}$

12.69   a. $F = 13,720.47$

   b.   Reject H_0.

   c.   Reject H_0.

   d.   *p*-value = .000; reject H_0.

   e. $(117.13)^2 = 13,720.47$ (within rounding error)

12.71   a. $F = 5.1817 / (.13435 / 4) = 154.279$

   b. $F_{.05} = 7.71$ $df_1 = 1, df_2 = 4$

   Since 154.279 > 7.71, reject H_0.

   c. $F_{.01} = 21.2$ $df_1 = 1, df_2 = 4$

   Since 154.279 > 21.2, reject H_0.

   d.   *p*-value =.0002; Reject H_0 at all levels of α

   e. $t^2 = (12.4209)^2 = 154.279$ (approximately equals F = 154.279)

   $(t_{.025})^2 = (2.776)^2 = 7.71 = F_{.05}$

12.73   Create a histogram, stem-and-leaf, and normal plot.

12.75   Approximate horizontal band appearance. No violations indicated

12.77   No.

12.79   The residual plot has somewhat of a cyclical appearance. Since d =.473 is less than $d_{L,.05} = 1.27$, we conclude there is positive autocorrelation and since 4 − .473 = 3.527 and this is greater than $d_{U,.05} = 1.45$ we conclude that there is not negative autocorrelation.

12.81   a.   Yes; see the plot in part c.

   b. $b_0 = 306.619, b_1 = -27.714$

c.　$\hat{y} = 306.619 - 27.714x$

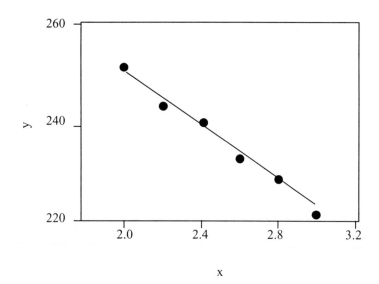

d.　p–value $= .000$, reject H_0, significant

e.　$x_0 = \$2.10;\ \hat{y} = 248.420;\ [244.511, 252.327]$
　　$x_0 = \$2.75;\ \hat{y} = 230.405;\ [226.697, 234.112]$
　　$x_0 = \$3.10;\ \hat{y} = 220.705;\ [216.415, 224.994]$

12.83　**a.**　No

　　b.　Possibly not; Don't take up smoking

12.85　From Minitab

```
The regression equation is
Market Rate = 0.85 + 0.610 Accounting Rate

Predictor        Coef      SE Coef          T         P
Constant        0.847        1.975       0.43     0.670
Accounti       0.6105       0.1431       4.27     0.000

Predicted Values for New Observations

New Obs     Fit      SE Fit         95.0% CI              95.0% PI
1        10.004      0.753    (  8.494,  11.514)  (  -0.310,  20.318)

Values of Predictors for New Observations

New Obs   Accounti
1             15.0
```

a.　$\hat{y} = b_0 + b_1(15.00) = .847 + .6105(15.00) = 10.0045$
　　95% C.I.: [8.494, 11.514]

b.　10.0045
　　95% P.I.: [−.310, 20.318]

12.87 **a.** There is a relationship since F = 21.13 with a *p*-value of .0002.

b. $b_1 = 35.2877$, [19.2202,51.3553]

12.89 $\hat{y} = 2.0572 + 6.3545(1/5) = 3.3281$

CHAPTER 13—Multiple Regression and Model Building

13.1 y is the dependent variable; $x_1, x_2, ...x_k$ are the independent variables or predictors.

13.3   Unknown regression parameters relating the mean value of y to $x_1, x_2, ..., x_k$.

13.5 β_0 is the mean value of y when all predictor variables equal zero. β_1 is the change in the mean of y associated with a one unit increase in x_1 when all other predictor variables stay the same.

13.7   **a.**   The plots show a linear (or somewhat linear) relationship between Price & Demand, IndPrice & Demand, and AdvExp & Demand.

   b.   The mean demand for the large size bottle of Fresh when the price of Fresh is $3.70, the average industry price of competitors' similar detergents is $3.90 and the advertising expenditure to promote Fresh is 6.50 ($650,000).

   c. β_0 = meaningless in practical terms

   β_1 = the mean change in demand for each additional dollar in the price of Fresh holding all other predictor variables constant.

   β_2 = the mean change in demand for each additional dollar in the average price of competitors' detergents holding all other predictor variables constant.

   β_3 = the mean change in demand for each additional $100,000 spent on advertising Fresh holding all other predictor variables constant.

   ϵ = all other factors that influence the demand for Fresh detergent

   d.   The plots for Demand vs. AdvExp and Demand vs. PriceDif appear to be more linear than the other two plots.

13.9   SSE

13.11   **a.** $b_0 = 29.347$, $b_1 = 5.6128$, $b_2 = 3.8344$

   b_0 = meaningless

   $b_1 = 5.6128$ implies that we estimate that mean sales price increases by $5,612.80 for each increase of 100 square feet in house size, when the niceness rating stays constant.

   $b_2 = 3.8344$ implies that we estimate that mean sales price increases by $3,834.40 for each increase in niceness rating of 1, when the square footage remains constant.

   b.   172.28. From $\hat{y} = 29.347 + 5.6128(20) + 3.8344(8)$

13.13   **a.** $b_0 = 1946.8020$, $b_1 = 0.0386$, $b_2 = 1.0394$, $b_0 = -413.7578$

   b. $\hat{y} = 15896.24725$, from $\hat{y} = 1946.802 + .03858 (56194) + 1.0394 (14077.88) - 413.7578$ $(6.89) = 15896.25$.

    c.   Therefore, actual hours were $17207.31 - 15896.25 = 1311.06$ hours greater than predicted.

13.15   **a.**   The proportion of the total variation in the observed values of the dependent variable explained by the multiple regression model.

    b.   The adjusted R-squared differs from R-squared by taking into consideration the number of independent variables in the model.

13.17   (1) $SSE = 73.6; s^2 = \dfrac{SSE}{n-(k+1)} = \dfrac{73.6}{10-(2+1)} = \dfrac{73.6}{7} = 10.5; s = \sqrt{10.5} = 3.242$

    (2)   Total variation $= 7447.5$
              Unexplained variation $= 73.6$
              Explained variation $= 7374$

    (3) $R^2 = \dfrac{7374}{7447.5} = .99 \qquad \overline{R}^2 = \left(R^2 - \dfrac{k}{n-1} \right)\left(\dfrac{n-1}{n-(k+1)} \right)$

$$= \left(.99 - \dfrac{2}{10-1} \right)\left(\dfrac{10-1}{10-(2+1)} \right)$$

$$= .987$$

            R^2 and $\overline{R}^2$ close together and close to 1.

    (4)   F(model) $= \dfrac{(\text{Explained variation})/k}{(\text{Unexplained variation})/(n-(k+1))}$

$$= \dfrac{7374/2}{73.6/(10-(2+1))} = \dfrac{7374/2}{73.6/7} = 350.87$$

    (5)   Based on 2 and 7 degrees of freedom, $F_{.05} = 4.74$. Since $F(\text{model}) = 350.87 > 4.74$, we reject $H_0 : \beta_1 = \beta_2 = 0$ by setting $\alpha = .05$.

    (6)   Based on 2 and 7 degrees of freedom, $F_{.01} = 9.55$. Since $F(\text{model}) = 350.87 > 9.55$, we reject $H_0 : \beta_1 = \beta_2 = 0$ by setting $\alpha = .01$.

    (7) p-value $= 0.00$ (which means less than .001). Since this p-value is less than $\alpha = .10, .05,$ .01, and .001, we have extremely strong evidence that $H_0 : \beta_1 = \beta_2 = 0$ is false. That is, we have extremely strong evidence that at least one of x_1 and x_2 is significantly related to y.

13.19   (1) $SSE = 1,798,712.2179$

$$s^2 = \dfrac{SSE}{n-(k+1)} = \dfrac{1,798,712.2179}{16-(3+1)} = 149892.68483$$

$$s = \sqrt{149892.68483} = 387.15977$$

(2) total variation = 464,126,601.6

unexplained = 1,798,712.2179

explained = 462,327,889.39

(3) $R^2 = \dfrac{462,327,889.39}{464,126,601.6} = .9961$

$$\overline{R}^2 = \left(R^2 - \frac{k}{n-1} \right)\left(\frac{n-1}{n-(k+1)} \right) = \left(.9961 - \frac{3}{16-1} \right)\left(\frac{16-1}{16-(3+1)} \right) = .9952$$

R^2 and $\overline{R}^2$ close to each other and 1.

(4) $F = \dfrac{(\text{Explained variation})/k}{(\text{Unexplained variation})/(n-(k+1))} = \dfrac{462,327,889.39/3}{1,798,712.2179/(16-(3+1))} = 1028.131$

(5) Based on 3 and 12 degrees of freedom, $F_{.05} = 3.49$

$F = 1028.131 > F_{.05} = 3.49$. Reject $H_0 : \beta_1 = \beta_2 = \beta_3 = 0$ at $\alpha = .05$

(6) Based on 3 and 12 degrees of freedom, $F_{.01} = 5.95$

$F = 1028.131 > F_{.01} = 5.95$. Reject $H_0 : \beta_1 = \beta_2 = \beta_3 = 0$ at $\alpha = .01$

(7) p-value = .0001. Reject H_0 at $\alpha = .05, .01,$ and $.001$.

13.21 Explanations will vary.

13.23 Works like Exercise 12.22

$y = \beta_0 + \beta_1 x_1 + \beta_2 x_2 + \beta_3 x_3 + \varepsilon$

$n - (k + 1) = 30 - (3 + 1) = 26$

Rejection points:

$t_{.025} = 2.056 \quad t_{.005} = 2.779$

$H_0: \beta_0 = 0 \qquad t = \dfrac{7.5891}{2.4450} = 3.104$; Reject H_0 at $\alpha = .05, \alpha = .01$

$H_0: \beta_1 = 0 \qquad t = \dfrac{-2.3577}{.6379} = -3.696$; Reject H_0 at $\alpha = .05$, not $.01$

$H_0: \beta_2 = 0 \qquad t = \dfrac{1.6122}{.2954} = 5.459$; Reject H_0 at $\alpha = .05, \alpha = .01$

$H_0: \beta_3 = 0 \qquad t = \dfrac{.5012}{.1259} = 3.981$; Reject H_0 at $\alpha = .05, \alpha = .01$

p-value for testing $H_0: \beta_1 = 0$ is $.001$; Reject H_0 at $\alpha = .01$

$H_0: \beta_2 = 0$ is less than $.001$; Reject H_0 at $\alpha = .001$

$$H_0: \beta_3 = 0 \text{ is }.0005; \text{ Reject } H_0 \text{ at } \alpha = .001$$

95% C.I.: $[b_j \pm 2.056\, s_{b_j}]$

99% C.I.: $[b_j \pm 2.779\, s_{b_j}]$

13.25 A measure of the distance of a particular set of values of the independent variables $x_1, x_2, ..., x_k$ from $(\bar{x}_1, \bar{x}_2, ..., \bar{x}_k)$, the averages of the previously observed values of $x_1, x_2, ..., x_k$.

13.27 **a.** Point estimate is $\hat{y} = 172.28$ ($172,280)

95% confidence interval is [168.56, 175.99]

b. Point prediction is $\hat{y} = 172.28$

95% prediction interval is [163.76, 180.80]

c. Stdev Fit = $s\sqrt{\text{Distance value}} = 1.57$

This implies that Distance value = $(1.57 / s)^2$

$= (1.57 / 3.242)^2$

$= 0.2345$

The 99% confidence interval for mean sales price is

$[\hat{y} \pm t_{.005}\, s\sqrt{\text{Distance value}}]$ with $t_{.005}$ based on 7 degrees of freedom

$= [172.28 \pm 3.499(1.57)]$

$= [172.28 \pm 5.49]$

$= [166.79, 177.77]$

The 99% prediction interval for an individual sales price is

$[\hat{y} \pm t_{.005}\, s\sqrt{1 + \text{Distance value}}]$

$= [172.28 \pm 3.499(3.242)\sqrt{1 + 0.2345}]$

$= [172.28 \pm 12.60]$

$= [159.68, 184.88]$

13.29 $y = 17207.31$ is above the upper limit of the interval [14906.2, 16886.3]; this y-value is unusually high.

13.31 See pages 572–579 in the text.

13.33 **a.** The pool coefficient is $25,862.30. Since the cost of the pool is $35,000 you expect to recoup $25,862.3 / $35,000 = 74%.

b. There is not an interaction between pool and any other independent variable.

13.35 **a.** The point estimate of the effect on the mean of campaign B compared to campaign A is $b_4 = 0.2695$.

The 95% confidence interval = [0.1262, 0.4128]

The point estimate of the effect on mean of campaign C compared to campaign A is $b_5 = 0.4396$.

The 95% confidence interval = [0.2944, 0.5847]

Campaign C is probably most effective even though intervals overlap.

b. $\hat{y} = 8.7154 - 2.768(3.7) + 1.6667(3.9) + 0.4927(6.5) + 0.4396 = 8.61621$

Confidence interval = [8.5138, 8.71862] Prediction interval = [8.28958, 8.94285]

c. β_5 = effect on mean of Campaign C compared to Campaign B.

d. β_5 is significant at alpha = 0.1 and alpha = 0.05 because *p*-value = 0.0179. Thus there is strong evidence that β_5 is greater than 0.

95% confidence interval= [0.0320, 0.3081], since it doesn't overlap 0, we are at least 95% confident that β_5 is greater than 0.

13.37 The situation in which the independent variables used in a regression analysis are related to each other.

Multicollinearity can affect the least squares point estimates, the standard errors of these estimates, and the t statistics. Multicollinearity can also cause combinations of values of the independent variables that one might expect to be in the experimental region to actually not be in this region.

13.39 **a.** $r_{x_1 x_3}, r_{x_1 x_4}, r_{x_3 x_4}$

VIF_1, VIF_3, VIF_4

b. x_1, x_3, x_4

c. b_1 and b_4

b. yes

c. Model 1; Model 2; Model 1; Model 2; Could choose either model, although Model 2 may be considered better because of the smaller C and *p*-value and because of the results of the stepwise regression and backward elimination.

13.41 By plotting the residuals against the values of each x_j, $\hat{y}$, and time (if the data are time series data). If the fitted model is appropriate, there will be no apparent pattern in the plots of the residuals. If there is a pattern, the model is not appropriate. To check the normality assumption, we construct a histogram, stem-and-leaf display, and normal plot of the residuals.

13.43 **a.** straight line appearance

b. explanations will vary

13.45 $\hat{y} = 30{,}626 + 3.893(28) - 29{,}607(1.56) + 86.52(1821.7) \cong 142{,}162$

13.47 Relating stock market return to credit rating (x_1) for emerging countries:

$\hat{y} = 56.9171 - 0.5574x_1 - 18.2934(0) + 0.3537x_1(0)\ \ 56.9171 - 0.5574x_1.$

For developing countries:

$\hat{y} = 56.9171 - 0.5574x_1 - 18.2934(1) + 0.3537x1(1)\ \ 38.6237 - 0.2037x_1$

The nature of the interaction is that the impact (slope) of credit rating is less severe in the case of developing countries.

13.49 $\ln y_{133} = 4.69618 + .0103075\,(133) + .01903 = 6.086108$

Point estimate: $e^{6.0861} = 439.7$

95% prediction interval: $[e^{5.96593},\ e^{6.20627}] = [389.92,\ 495.85]$

13.51 **a.** Both terms have small p-values so both terms are significant so both are important.